This book belongs to:

EDITORIAL STAFF
Vice President and Editor-in-Chief: Anne Van Wagner Childs
Executive Director: Sandra Graham Case
Design Director: Patricia Wallenfang Sowers
Test Kitchen Director/Foods Editor: Celia Fahr Harkey, R.D.
Editorial Director: Susan Frantz Wiles
Publications Director: Kristine Anderson Mertes
Creative Art Director: Gloria Bearden

DESIGN
Designers: Polly Tullis Browning, Diana Sanders Cates, Cherece Athy Cooper, Cyndi Hansen, Sandra Spotts Ritchie, Billie Steward, Anne Pulliam Stocks, and Linda Diehl Tiano
Executive Assistant: Debra Smith

FOODS
Assistant Foods Editor: Jane Kenner Prather
Foods Copy Editor: Judy Millard
Test Kitchen Home Economists: Pat Coker and Rose Glass Klein
Test Kitchen Coordinator: Nora Faye Taylor
Test Kitchen Assistants: Brandy Black Alewine and Donna Huffner Spencer

TECHNICAL
Managing Editor: Barbara Marguerite McClintock
Senior Technical Writer: Theresa Hicks Young
Technical Writers: Jennifer Potts Hutchings, Susan McManus Johnson, and Kimberly J. Smith
Technical Associate: Candice Treat Murphy
Copy Editor: Susan Frazier
Technical Assistant: Sharon Gillam

EDITORIAL
Managing Editor: Linda L. Trimble
Associate Editors: Shelby D. Brewer, Darla Burdette Kelsay, Stacey Robertson Marshall, Suzie Puckett, and Hope Turner

ART
Book/Magazine Graphic Art Director: Diane Thomas
Graphic Artist: Mark R. Potter
Color Technician: Mark Hawkins
Staff Photographer: Russell Ganser
Photography Stylist: Karen Smart Hall
Publishing Systems Administrator: Becky Riddle
Publishing Systems Assistants: Myra S. Means and Chris Wertenberger

PROMOTIONS
Managing Editor: Alan Caudle
Associate Editor: Steven M. Cooper
Designer: Dale Rowett
Art Operations Director: Jeff Curtis
Graphic Artist: Deborah Kelly

BUSINESS STAFF
Publisher: Rick Barton
Vice President, Finance: Tom Siebenmorgen
Vice President, Retail Marketing: Bob Humphrey
Director of Corporate Planning and Development: Laticia Mull Cornett
Vice President, National Accounts: Pam Stebbins
Retail Marketing Director: Margaret Sweetin
General Merchandise Manager: Cathy Laird
Vice President, Operations: Jim Dittrich
Distribution Director: Rob Thieme
Retail Customer Service Manager: Wanda Price
Print Production Manager: Fred F. Pruss

Library of Congress Catalog Number 98-67372
International Standard Book Number 1-57486-166-2

10 9 8 7 6 5

CHRISTMAS GIFTS OF GOOD TASTE

Good food and festive gifts that delight family and friends — these are things we love about Christmas and other special days. That's why we're pleased to present this new edition of Christmas Gifts of Good Taste. It brings you over 100 yummy recipes for crunchy snacks, hearty soups, fresh-baked breads, and lots of sumptuous sweets to tantalize the taste buds of everyone on your gift list! And all are presented with creative craft ideas for keepsake containers or wrappings so your food gifts will be unforgettable! Christmas is the main focus of the book, but there also are gift ideas to help you mark Valentine's Day, Easter, Halloween, Thanksgiving, and other memorable days throughout the year. Many of our incredible edibles are quick to prepare, too — just look for the "Easy" emblem near the project title. The next time you need a creative and fun gift, let this collection be your guide! And remember: If it's homemade, it's from the heart!

Anne Childs

LEISURE ARTS, INC.
Little Rock, Arkansas

Table of Contents

WINTER WARM-UP

*H*elp your friends warm up after a cold day in the snow with a cup of hot cocoa
and a brightly decorated Snowman Cookie. Paint simple phrases and designs on ceramic
mugs to hold the yummy cookies, marshmallows, and packages of instant cocoa mix.
Gather the goodies in cellophane and pass them out with your best holiday wishes.

SNOWMAN COOKIES

*Positioning the arms and legs on the
snowmen before baking gives each its
own personality!*

COOKIES

- 3/4 cup butter or margarine, softened
- 1 package (3 ounces) cream cheese, softened
- 1 cup granulated sugar
- 1/2 cup confectioners sugar
- 1 egg
- 1 teaspoon almond extract
- 2 3/4 cups all-purpose flour
- 1/2 teaspoon baking powder
- 1/4 teaspoon salt

ICING

- 2 1/2 cups confectioners sugar
- 3 1/2 to 4 tablespoons milk
- 1/2 teaspoon almond extract
  Green, black, orange, and red paste food coloring

Preheat oven to 375 degrees. For
cookies, cream butter, cream cheese, and
sugars in a large bowl until fluffy. Add egg
and almond extract; beat until smooth. In
a medium bowl, combine flour, baking
powder, and salt. Add dry ingredients to
creamed mixture; stir until a soft dough
forms. On a lightly floured surface, use a
floured rolling pin to roll out dough to
3/8-inch thickness. Use a 4 1/4 x 5 1/4-inch
gingerbread boy cookie cutter to cut out
cookies. Place 2 inches apart on a lightly
greased baking sheet. Carefully move
arms and legs into different positions.
Bake 8 to 10 minutes or until bottoms are
lightly browned. Cool cookies on baking
sheet 2 minutes; transfer to a wire rack to
cool completely.

For icing, combine confectioners sugar,
milk, and almond extract in a small bowl;
stir until smooth. Transfer 3 tablespoons
icing into each of 3 small bowls; tint
green, black, and orange. Tint remaining
icing red. Spoon icing into pastry bags
fitted with small round tips. Use black
icing to pipe eyes and mouths onto
cookies. Use orange icing to pipe "carrot"
noses. Use red icing to pipe scarves and
boots. Use green icing to pipe mittens and
buttons. Let icing harden. Store in a single
layer between sheets of waxed paper in an
airtight container.

Yield: about 1 dozen cookies

SNOWMAN MUGS

For each mug, you will need a white
ceramic mug; rubbing alcohol; tracing
paper; transfer paper; red and green
fine-point paint pens; 24" square of clear
cellophane; rubber band; and white, red,
and green 1/4"w curling ribbons.

1. Wipe areas on mug to be painted with
alcohol; allow to dry.
2. Trace design, page 145, onto tracing
paper. Use transfer paper to transfer
design to mug. Use paint pens to draw
over design and draw borders above and
below design; allow to dry.
3. Place gift in mug. Center mug on
cellophane. Gather cellophane over mug;
secure with rubber band. Tie several 24"
lengths of curling ribbons into a bow
around gathers, covering rubber band.
Curl ribbon ends.
4. Hand wash mug in warm soapy water.

OH, CHRISTMAS TREES!

A classic taste of the Yuletide, these refreshing minty confections will be a sweet surprise for friends and family! The homemade candies — shaped like tiny Christmas trees — bring glad tidings when presented in a hanging basket embellished with faux greenery, holly, and cheery Christmas bows.

TINY PEPPERMINT TREES

- 3 cups confectioners sugar, divided
- 4 teaspoons meringue powder
- 2^1/$_2$ tablespoons water
- ^{1}/$_2$ teaspoon peppermint extract
  Green paste food coloring
  Confectioners sugar

In a large bowl, combine 1^1/$_2$ cups confectioners sugar, meringue powder, water, peppermint extract, and food coloring. Beat on low speed of an electric mixer until smooth. Gradually beat in remaining 1^1/$_2$ cups confectioners sugar, kneading by hand if necessary. Knead about 5 minutes or until candy is very smooth and no longer sticky. Sprinkle a small amount of confectioners sugar on a flat surface. Working with half of candy mixture at a time, use a rolling pin coated with confectioners sugar to roll out candy on sugar-coated surface to about ^{1}/$_4$-inch thickness. Use a 1^1/$_2$-inch tree-shaped cookie cutter to cut out candies. Place on a waxed paper-lined baking sheet. Loosely cover candies with waxed paper; let dry at room temperature overnight. Store in an airtight container.

Yield: about 5^1/$_2$ dozen candies

HOLLY BASKET

You will need a hanging basket (we used a 4^3/$_4$" square basket with leather hanger), 1^1/$_2$"w wired ribbon, hot glue gun, artificial greenery, two artificial holly sprigs with berries, 8" of craft wire, jar with lid to fit in basket (we used a quart jar with cork stopper), and natural excelsior.

1. Measure around rim of basket; add 6". Cut a length of ribbon the determined measurement. Tie ribbon into a knot at front of basket. Glue greenery and one holly sprig to front of basket.

2. Cut a 32" length of ribbon. Follow *Making a Bow*, page 153, to make a bow with six 4" loops and two 3" streamers. Use wire to attach bow to knot of first ribbon.

3. For jar topper, measure around lid; add ^{1}/$_2$". Cut a length of ribbon the determined measurement. Glue ribbon around lid; glue remaining holly sprig to ribbon.

4. Line basket with excelsior. Place jar in basket.

SIMPLE GOODNESS

*T*his Christmas, give the hearty goodness of our ready-to-eat Baked Chicken Stew to a busy family. Healthy fixings such as chicken, carrots, and potatoes make this a wholesome meal that's sure to beat the chills! Carry the savory creation in a basket lined with a red-checked kitchen towel; accent with holly candle rings for a festive touch.

BAKED CHICKEN STEW

1	can (14$^{1}/_{2}$ ounces) chicken broth
1	can (10 ounces) diced tomatoes and green chiles
2	tablespoons cornstarch
2	teaspoons sugar
1$^{1}/_{2}$	teaspoons salt
1	teaspoon lemon pepper
1$^{1}/_{4}$	pounds boneless skinless chicken breasts, cut into 1-inch pieces
1$^{1}/_{2}$	cups thickly sliced carrots
4	cups cubed potatoes
1$^{1}/_{2}$	cups 1-inch celery pieces
1	large onion, coarsely chopped

Preheat oven to 375 degrees. In a large bowl, combine chicken broth, tomatoes and green chiles, cornstarch, sugar, salt, and lemon pepper. Stir in chicken, carrots, potatoes, celery, and onion. Place mixture in a greased 9 x 13-inch baking dish. Cover and bake 1$^{1}/_{2}$ to 2 hours or until meat and vegetables are tender. Serve warm.

Yield: about 6 servings

CASSEROLE LINER

You will need an 18" x 24" kitchen towel for liner, 15" x 10" x 3" basket, 9" x 13" casserole dish, two rubber bands, and two 1$^{1}/_{2}$" dia. candle rings with artificial holly leaves and berries.

With short ends of towel extending beyond short ends of basket and folding long edges to wrong side as necessary, place liner, then dish in basket. Gather each short end of liner close to basket; secure with rubber bands. Place one candle ring over each rubber band.

JOLLY JAM

*T*is the season for spreading peace and goodwill — and with our Strawberry-Banana Jam, you can spread sweet greetings, too! The fruity preserves are guaranteed to delight everyone on your list. Top a jar of the jam with a delicate doily and place in a beribboned basket. Include some muffins for a treat that's ready to eat.

STRAWBERRY-BANANA JAM

 1 package (20 ounces) frozen whole strawberries, thawed and crushed
 1½ cups mashed bananas (about 4 bananas)
 3 tablespoons freshly squeezed lemon juice
 1 package (1¾ ounces) powdered fruit pectin
 5 cups sugar

In a Dutch oven, combine strawberries, bananas, lemon juice, and pectin over medium-high heat. Stirring constantly, bring to a rolling boil. Add sugar. Stirring constantly, bring to a rolling boil again and boil 1 minute. Remove from heat; skim off foam. Pour jam into heat-resistant jars; cover and cool to room temperature. Store in refrigerator.

Yield: about 3 pints jam

LINER AND LACE JAR LID COVER

You will need an 8" dia. Battenberg lace doily, rubber band, ¼"w satin ribbon, hot glue gun, holly berry sprig, fabric for liner and bow, and a basket (we used a 7" x 9" oval basket with handle).

1. Center doily over jar lid (from recipe this page); secure with rubber band. Measure around lid; add 10". Cut a length from ribbon the determined measurement. Tie ribbon into a bow around jar, covering rubber band. Glue berry sprig to knot of bow.

2. Use fabric for liner and follow *Making a Basket Liner*, page 152, to make a liner with finished edges.
3. Measure around basket; add 18". Tear a 2½"w strip from fabric for bow the determined measurement. Tie strip into a bow around basket.
4. Place liner and gift in basket.

CAJUN SENSATION

*P*erk up plain popcorn
with our Bayou Popcorn Spice!
This Cajun sensation can be
concocted in seconds: simply blend
all the sassy spices together and
pack with a bag of microwave
popcorn. Add a handmade label
and then "pop" in on friends —
everyone will love the zesty taste.

BAYOU POPCORN SPICE

     3 tablespoons paprika
     1 tablespoon garlic powder
     2 teaspoons onion powder
 1¹/₂ teaspoons ground red pepper
     1 teaspoon dried thyme leaves
     1 teaspoon dried oregano leaves
     1 teaspoon brown sugar
     1 teaspoon ground black pepper
  ¹/₂ teaspoon ground nutmeg
       Microwave popcorn to give

In a small bowl, combine all
ingredients until well blended. Store in an
airtight container. Give with popcorn and
serving instructions.

Yield: about 7 tablespoons mix

To serve: Microwave a 3¹/₂-ounce bag of
microwave popcorn according to package
directions. Open bag carefully to avoid
steam. Sprinkle ¹/₂ to 1 teaspoon
seasoning mix, or more to taste, over
popcorn. Hold top of bag closed and
shake until popcorn is coated.

POPCORN SEASONING BAG

You will need a brown lunch-size paper
bag, craft glue stick, decorative-edge craft
scissors, stapler, colored pencils, and a
photocopy of label design (page 150) on
ecru card stock.

1. With bag folded, glue bottom of bag in
place. Use craft scissors to trim top of
bag. Place popcorn and seasoning mix in
bag. Fold top of bag 1¹/₂" to front; staple
through center folded portion to secure.
2. Use pencils to color label. Leaving a
¹/₂"w border, use craft scissors to cut out
label. Glue label to bag.

CHRISTMAS COCOA

*N*othing can beat a cup
of steaming hot cocoa on a
cold winter's night! We've added
the surprise flavor of crushed
peppermint candies to Triple
Chocolate-Mint Cocoa Mix for
a gourmet taste. Decorate papier-
mâché boxes to resemble pinwheel
peppermints and wrap them in
cellophane for the perfect finish.

TRIPLE CHOCOLATE-MINT COCOA MIX

*Candies can be ground in a coffee mill
or crushed with a hammer.*

    6 cups nonfat milk powder
    1 package (16 ounces) confectioners
         sugar
    2 jars (8 ounces each) Swiss
         chocolate-flavored non-dairy
         powdered creamer
    1 package (15 ounces) chocolate mix
         for milk
    1 package (7½ ounces) round
         peppermint candies, finely
         ground
    ¼ cup unsweetened cocoa powder
    1 teaspoon salt

In a very large bowl, combine milk
powder, confectioners sugar, creamer,
chocolate mix, ground candies, cocoa,
and salt. Store in an airtight container in
refrigerator. Give with serving instructions.

Yield: about 13½ cups cocoa mix

To serve: Pour 6 ounces hot water over
3 tablespoons cocoa mix; stir until well
blended.

PEPPERMINT BOXES

For each box, you will need a 4⅜" dia.
papier-mâché box, white and red acrylic
paint, paintbrushes, tracing paper,
transfer paper, pencil, paper towel, green
and black permanent fine-point markers,
6" x 12" clear cellophane bag, and two
6" lengths of ¹⁄₁₆"w satin ribbon.

*Allow paint to dry after each
application.*

1. Remove lid from box. Paint box and
lid white.
2. Trace swirl design, page 139, onto
tracing paper. Use transfer paper to
transfer design to top of lid. Place lid on
box. Using pencil, refer to Diagram to
extend lines from top of lid onto sides of
lid and box.
3. Paint alternate sections red. To
highlight one side of each red section, dip
side of a flat brush in white paint and

wipe brush on paper towel until almost
dry; pull brush along edge of red section.
Use black marker to outline red sections.
Use green marker to draw one line down
center of each white section.
4. Place bag of cocoa mix inside box;
replace lid on box. Trim bottom from
cellophane bag. Center box inside bag.
Gather each end of bag at each side of
box. Tie one ribbon length into a bow at
each end of box, covering gathers.

Diagram

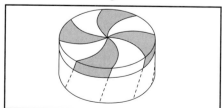

SPREADING CHEER

*T*his year, why not "spread" some holiday cheer with our Creamy Orange Bagel Spread! Sweet and tempting, this topping is as easy to prepare as it is delicious. Make a neighbor feel special by presenting the gift in Santa-face bags cleverly made from kitchen towels. It'll be a jolly way to start the day!

CREAMY ORANGE BAGEL SPREAD

   1 package (8 ounces) cream cheese, softened
1½ tablespoons orange juice
 ½ teaspoon orange extract
 ¾ cup confectioners sugar
     Bagels to serve

In a medium bowl, beat cream cheese until fluffy. Add orange juice and orange extract. Gradually beat in confectioners sugar. Store in an airtight container in refrigerator. Serve with bagels.

Yield: about 1⅓ cups spread

SANTA-FACE TOWEL BAGS

For each bag, you will need a 20" x 30" red-and-white striped kitchen towel; paper-backed fusible web; white, flesh, and red felt; transfer paper; clear nylon thread; red and black permanent fine-point markers; red 12mm wooden bead; ½" dia. jingle bell; and 30" of ⅝"w red satin wired ribbon.

1. Matching wrong sides and short edges, fold towel in half.
2. Use patterns, page 134, and follow *Making Appliqués*, page 152, to make hat appliqué from red felt; face appliqué from

flesh felt; and hair, mustache, and beard appliqués from white felt. Use transfer paper to transfer eyes to face appliqué.
3. Measuring 2½" from fold and overlapping appliqués as necessary, center and fuse appliqués on one side of towel. Use nylon thread and follow *Machine Appliqué*, page 154, to stitch around edges of appliqués.

4. Use red marker to lightly add cheeks and black marker to draw over eyes on Santa. Stitch bead to face for nose and bell to tip of hat.
5. Use towel and follow Steps 2, 3, and 5 of *Making a Fabric Bag*, page 154, to make a bag with a square bottom.
6. Place gift in bag. Tie ribbon into a bow around top of bag.

"DILL-ICIOUS" PRETZELS

To give ordinary pretzels a "twist," we've added the tart taste of dill! Our soft and chewy Yeasty Dill Pretzels are sure to wake up taste buds throughout the holiday season. Carry the salty treats in a basket embellished with a cross-stitched angel ornament.

YEASTY DILL PRETZELS

- 1 cup milk
- 1/2 cup chopped fresh dill weed, divided
- 2 tablespoons butter or margarine
- 1 package dry yeast
- 1 tablespoon sugar
- 1/2 cup warm water
- 3 3/4 to 4 1/4 cups all-purpose flour, divided
- 1 teaspoon salt
  Vegetable oil cooking spray
- 1 egg, lightly beaten
- 1 tablespoon water
- 2 teaspoons coarse salt

In a small saucepan over medium heat, combine milk, 1/3 cup dill weed, and butter. Heat just until butter melts; remove from heat and cool to lukewarm.

In a small bowl, dissolve yeast and sugar in 1/2 cup warm water. In a large bowl, combine 3 3/4 cups flour and 1 teaspoon salt. Add milk mixture and yeast mixture to dry ingredients; stir until a soft dough forms. Turn dough onto a lightly floured surface. Knead about 5 minutes or until dough becomes smooth and elastic, using additional flour as necessary. Place in a large bowl sprayed with cooking spray, turning once to coat top of dough. Cover and let rise in a warm place (80 to 85 degrees) 1 hour or until doubled in size.

Turn dough onto a lightly floured surface and punch down. Separate into 16 equal pieces. Roll each piece into a 20-inch-long rope. Shape each rope into a pretzel knot. Place 2 inches apart on lightly greased baking sheets. Spray tops of pretzels with cooking spray, cover, and let rise in a warm place 20 minutes.

Preheat oven to 375 degrees. In a small bowl, combine egg and 1 tablespoon water. Brush pretzels with egg mixture; sprinkle with remaining dill weed and coarse salt. Bake 17 to 19 minutes or until golden brown. Serve warm or transfer to a wire rack to cool. Store in an airtight container.

Yield: 16 pretzels

ANGEL ORNAMENT BASKET

You will need embroidery floss (see color key, page 141), two 7" squares of white Aida (14 ct), drawing compass, tracing paper, lightweight cardboard, low-loft polyester batting, hot glue gun, 18" of 1/4" dia. welting with lip, 1"w grosgrain ribbon, basket with handle (we used an 8" x 13" basket), two artificial pine sprigs with holly and berries, and fabric for basket liner.

Refer to Cross Stitch, page 151, before beginning project.

1. Using three strands of floss for *Cross Stitches* and one strand of floss for *Backstitches* and *French Knots*, center and stitch design, page 141, on one Aida square.

2. For pattern, use compass to draw a 3 5/8" dia. circle on tracing paper; cut out. Draw around pattern twice on cardboard and twice on batting; cut out. Center pattern over stitched piece; cut out stitched piece 1/2" larger than pattern. Cut a piece for backing from remaining Aida square the same size as stitched piece.

3. For ornament front, place stitched piece, right side down, on a flat surface. Center and layer one batting circle, then one cardboard circle on stitched piece. Clipping as necessary, fold and glue edges of stitched piece to back of cardboard. Repeat with backing fabric and remaining batting circle and cardboard for ornament back.

4. Beginning and ending at center bottom, follow *Adding Welting*, page 151, to glue lip of welting along back edges of ornament front.

5. Matching wrong sides, glue ornament front and back together.

6. Trimming to fit and overlapping ends at front, glue a length of ribbon around rim of basket. Glue pine sprigs and ornament over overlap of ribbon.

7. For basket liner, use fabric and follow *Making a Basket Liner*, page 152, to make a liner with unfinished edges.

8. Place liner and gift in basket.

NUTTY NOEL

A cinch to prepare, our Three-Pepper Nuts are made just as their name suggests — with a spicy blend of red, black, and white ground pepper. They're an absolute delight for nut lovers! Package these tidbits in a fun and festive Santa bag adorned with a Yuletide bow.

THREE-PEPPER NUTS

    2 cups pecan halves
    2 cups walnut halves
    2 cups whole almonds
  1/2 cup butter or margarine, melted
    1 tablespoon white wine
         Worcestershire sauce
 1 1/2 teaspoons salt
    1 teaspoon ground red pepper
    1 teaspoon ground black pepper
    1 teaspoon ground white pepper

Preheat oven to 300 degrees. Place nuts in a 9 x 13-inch baking pan. In a small bowl, combine melted butter, white wine Worcestershire sauce, salt, and peppers. Pour mixture over nuts; stir to coat. Bake 30 minutes, stirring every 10 minutes. Cool in pan. Store in an airtight container.

Yield: about 6 cups nuts

ELFIN SANTA BAG

You will need two 3³/₄" high wooden doll pins; red acrylic paint; paintbrush; white chenille stem; tracing paper; white, red, and tan craft foam; low-temperature glue gun; hole punch; pink card stock; craft glue stick; black permanent fine-point marker; brown lunch-size paper bag; and 18" of 1¹/₂"w wired ribbon.

Use low-temperature glue gun for all gluing unless otherwise indicated.

1. For arms, leaving ball of each pin unpainted, paint pins red; allow to dry. Cut chenille stem in half. Wrap one stem half around each "wrist" for "cuffs."
2. Trace patterns, page 139, onto tracing paper; cut out. Draw around patterns and cut out head from tan foam; hat from red foam; and beard, "pom-pom," and hat brim from white foam.
3. Arrange and glue foam pieces on head. Use hole punch to punch two pink "cheeks" from card stock; use glue stick to glue cheeks on face. Use marker to draw face on head.
4. Place gift in bag. Fold bag ¹/₂", then 1¹/₂" to front; slide arms over fold to secure. Tie ribbon into a bow; glue at top of bag. Glue head at top of bag.

EASY CHEESY BISCUITS

Need a last-minute gift in a hurry? Our Cheddar-Garlic Biscuit Mix can be made in minutes with ingredients you may already have on hand! It's even easy to prepare — just add milk and bake a batch of the tasty treats. Place the flavorful mix in a handmade calico bag that's embellished with a button "tree" and red raffia tie.

CHEDDAR-GARLIC BISCUIT MIX

    4 cups all-purpose baking mix
    2 cups (8 ounces) shredded sharp
       Cheddar cheese
    2 teaspoons garlic powder
    2 teaspoons dried Italian herb
       seasoning

In a large bowl, combine baking mix, cheese, garlic powder, and Italian seasoning. Divide mix in half. Place each half in a resealable plastic bag. Store in refrigerator. Give with serving instructions.

Yield: about 5 cups biscuit mix, about 2¹/₂ cups each bag

To serve: Store biscuit mix in refrigerator until ready to prepare. Preheat oven to 425 degrees. Place mix (about 2¹/₂ cups) in a medium bowl. Add ³/₄ cup milk; stir until well blended. On a lightly floured surface, use a floured rolling pin to roll out dough to ¹/₂-inch thickness. Use a 2-inch-diameter biscuit cutter to cut out biscuits. Transfer to a greased baking sheet. Bake 11 to 13 minutes or until golden brown. Brush with melted butter. Serve warm.

Yield: about 1¹/₂ dozen biscuits

BUTTON BAGS

For each bag, you will need a 14" x 16" piece of fabric, hot glue gun, assorted buttons, and several 24" lengths of raffia.

1. Use fabric and follow steps 2 - 5 of *Making a Fabric Bag,* page 154, to make bag.

2. Arrange and glue buttons into a tree shape on front of bag.
3. Place gift in bag. Tie raffia together into a bow around top of bag.

SNOW-CAPPED MUNCHIES

*S*anta can't compete with these sensational sweets! Our Chocolate Rice Bites are "snow-capped" treasures that combine the tantalizing taste of chocolate with a crunch that's out of this world! Make a co-worker's day by delivering the munchables in a bright red gift bag topped off with a jolly Santa.

CHOCOLATE RICE BITES

- 1 package (12 ounces) square rice cereal
- 1 package (12 ounces) semisweet chocolate chips
- 1/4 cup butter or margarine
- 2 tablespoons chocolate syrup
- 1 teaspoon vanilla extract
- 3 1/2 cups confectioners sugar, divided

Place cereal in a very large lightly greased bowl. In a medium saucepan, combine chocolate chips, butter, and chocolate syrup. Stirring constantly, cook over low heat until chocolate chips melt and mixture is smooth. Stir in vanilla. Pour over cereal in bowl; stir to evenly coat. In a 2-gallon resealable bag, combine 2 1/2 cups confectioners sugar and coated cereal. Seal and shake bag to evenly coat cereal with sugar. Spread on aluminum foil; let stand 30 minutes. Return cereal to bag with remaining 1 cup confectioners sugar. Seal and shake bag to coat cereal again. Store in an airtight container.

Yield: about 15 cups snack mix

SANTA LABEL BAG

You will need a 5" x 7" gift bag, stapler, 8" of 1"w grosgrain ribbon, hot glue gun, colored pencils, photocopy of label design (page 150) on white card stock, and a red permanent fine-point marker.

1. Place gift in bag. Fold top of bag 1" to front twice; staple through center folded portion to secure.

2. Fold ribbon into a "V" shape; staple at top of bag.

3. Use pencils to color label. Use marker to write message on label. Leaving a 1/8" border, cut out label. Glue label at top of bag.

CHRISTMAS RELISH

*R*eward your dearest friends with something they can relish! Great for adding zip to favorite dishes, our Christmas Squash Relish is simple to prepare, and it's packed with flavor. Deliver the zesty condiment in a cross-stitched snowman bag.

CHRISTMAS SQUASH RELISH

- 10 cups coarsely chopped fresh yellow squash (about 3 pounds)
- 4 cups coarsely chopped onions (about 1½ pounds)
- 2 sweet red peppers, coarsely chopped (about 4 cups)
- 2 green peppers, coarsely chopped (about 3 cups)
- 4 jalapeño peppers, seeded and coarsely chopped
- 3 tablespoons plus 1 teaspoon canning and pickling salt, divided
- 4 cups sugar
- 2½ cups apple cider vinegar
- 2 tablespoons cornstarch
- 1 teaspoon ground black pepper
- 1 teaspoon ground nutmeg
- 1 teaspoon ground turmeric

Process vegetables in batches in a food processor until finely chopped. Place in a very large bowl. Stir in 3 tablespoons salt. Cover top of vegetables with ice. Cover bowl and refrigerate overnight.

Rinse vegetables with cold water and drain. In a large non-aluminum Dutch oven, combine vegetables, sugar, vinegar, cornstarch, remaining teaspoon salt, black pepper, nutmeg, and turmeric. Stirring occasionally, bring to a boil over medium heat. Boil uncovered 30 minutes. Spoon into heat-resistant jars; cover and

cool to room temperature. Store in refrigerator.

Yield: about 12 cups relish

CROSS-STITCHED SNOWMAN BAG

You will need embroidery floss (see color key, page 142), white Lil Tote™ (14 ct), fabric for lid cover, pinking shears, rubber band, and white and red curling ribbons.

Refer to Cross Stitch, page 151, before beginning project.

1. Using three strands of floss for *Cross Stitches* and one strand of floss for *Backstitches* and *French Knots,* center and stitch snowman design, page 142, on front of bag with top of design 1½" from bottom edge.

2. For jar lid cover, draw around jar lid (from recipe this page) on wrong side of fabric. Use pinking shears to cut out circle 2" outside drawn line. Place circle over lid; secure with rubber band. Knot curling ribbons around lid, covering rubber band. Curl ribbon ends.

Make someone's Christmas a bit more flavorful with our Red Onion Jelly! Sweet and savory, this delicious delicacy boasts a one-of-a-kind flavor that's great with crackers or even as a meat glaze. Snuggle jars of the jelly in poinsettia-trimmed baskets for perfectly pleasing gifts!

RED ONION JELLY

    4   cups chopped red onions
  2³/4   cups apple juice
    2   tablespoons freshly squeezed lemon
          juice
    1   package (1³/4 ounces) powdered
          fruit pectin
  5¹/2   cups sugar
          Red liquid food coloring
          (optional)

In a Dutch oven, combine onions, apple juice, lemon juice, and pectin over medium-high heat. Stirring constantly, bring to a rolling boil. Add sugar. Stirring constantly, bring to a rolling boil again and boil 1 minute. Remove from heat; skim off foam. Strain mixture, discarding onions. Tint red, if desired. Spoon jelly into heat-resistant jars; cover and cool to room temperature. Store in refrigerator. Serve with cream cheese and crackers or use as a meat glaze.

Yield: about 7 half-pints of jelly

POINSETTIA BASKETS

For each basket, you will need pinking shears, fabric, ¹/8"w gold ribbon, hot glue gun, small artificial poinsettia pick, and a basket large enough to accommodate jar (we used a 3³/4" hexagon-shaped basket).

1. Measure across widest part of jar lid (from recipe this page); add 2". Use pinking shears to cut a square from fabric the determined measurement. Center square over lid.

2. Leaving extra long streamers, knot ribbon around lid.
3. Glue pick to front of basket. Place jar in basket.

22

NOT YOUR ORDINARY BRITTLE

*A*dd a touch of lemon to an old favorite and what do you get? An unforgettable taste sensation! Our Lemon-Pecan Brittle is a cheery way to say "Happy Holidays" to your loved ones. Wrap up the crunchy confections in an appliquéd poinsettia bag. What a sweet treat indeed!

LEMON-PECAN BRITTLE

- 2 cups sugar
- 1/2 cup light corn syrup
- 1/3 cup water
- 1/4 teaspoon salt
- 1 1/2 cups chopped pecans
- 3 tablespoons butter or margarine
- 1 teaspoon lemon extract
- 1 teaspoon grated lemon zest
- 1 teaspoon baking soda

Butter sides of a heavy large saucepan. Combine sugar, corn syrup, water, and salt in saucepan. Stirring constantly, cook over medium-low heat until sugar dissolves. Using a pastry brush dipped in hot water, wash down any sugar crystals on sides of pan. Attach a candy thermometer to pan, making sure thermometer does not touch bottom of pan. Increase heat to medium and bring to a boil. Cook, without stirring, about 8 minutes or until mixture reaches 260 degrees. Stir in pecans and continue cooking until mixture reaches hard-crack stage (approximately 300 to 310 degrees). Test about 1/2 teaspoon mixture in ice water. Mixture will form brittle threads in ice water and will remain brittle when removed from water. Remove from heat and add butter, lemon extract, and lemon zest. Stir until butter

melts. Stir in baking soda (mixture will foam). Pour candy onto a large piece of greased aluminum foil placed on a dampened flat surface. For thinner brittle, place 1 rubber spatula on top and a second spatula underneath. Lift edges of brittle and stretch as brittle cools. Cool completely. Break into pieces. Store in an airtight container.

Yield: about 1 1/2 pounds brittle

APPLIQUÉD POINSETTIA BAG

You will need paper-backed fusible web, red and green fabrics, 7 3/4" x 11 1/2" canvas bag, tracing paper, transfer paper, black permanent fine-point marker, hot glue gun, six 3/8" dia. yellow buttons, and 24" of 1 1/2"w wired ribbon.

1. Use patterns, page 140, and follow *Making Appliqués*, page 152, to make one each of small poinsettia, large poinsettia, leaf A, and leaf B appliqués from fabrics. Arrange and fuse appliqués on bag.
2. Trace "Happy Holidays" pattern, page 140, onto tracing paper. Use transfer paper to transfer words to bag. Use marker to draw dashes along edges of poinsettias and down center of each leaf, draw curly vines and dots, and draw over words on bag.
3. Arrange and glue buttons to center of poinsettia.
4. Place gift in bag. Tie ribbon into a bow around top of bag.

WARM CHRISTMAS WISHES

Greet friends or family with warmest wishes of the Christmas season. Our Artichoke and Roasted Red Pepper Dip is ready for folks to heat and eat — you even provide the crackers! Deliver your Yuletide appetizer in a basket lined with a folksy appliquéd cloth, complete with baking instructions and a festive bow.

ARTICHOKE AND ROASTED RED PEPPER DIP

- 2 large sweet red peppers
- 1/4 cup sliced green onions
- 2 tablespoons butter or margarine
- 1 can (14 ounces) artichoke hearts, drained and chopped
- 1 1/4 cups freshly grated Parmesan cheese, divided
- 1 cup mayonnaise
- 1/2 cup sour cream
- 1/4 teaspoon salt
- 1/8 teaspoon ground red pepper
  Green onion to garnish
  Crackers to serve

To roast sweet red peppers, cut in half lengthwise and remove seeds and membranes. Place, skin side up, on an ungreased baking sheet; flatten peppers with hand. Broil about 3 inches from heat about 10 minutes or until peppers are blackened. Immediately seal peppers in a plastic bag and allow to steam 10 to 15 minutes. Remove and discard charred skin; coarsely chop peppers.

In a medium skillet over medium heat, cook 1/4 cup green onions in butter until tender. Remove from heat. Stir in artichoke hearts, 1 cup Parmesan cheese, mayonnaise, sour cream, salt, ground red pepper, and roasted peppers. Transfer to

3 greased 1 1/4-cup ramekins. Garnish with remaining 1/4 cup Parmesan cheese and green onion. Cover and store in refrigerator. Give with crackers and serving instructions.

Yield: about 3 1/4 cups dip

To serve: Bake uncovered dip in a 350-degree oven 25 minutes or until heated through. Serve warm with crackers or bread.

BASKET LINER AND RECIPE CARD

You will need fabric for liner and stars, basket with handle (we used a 7" x 15" basket), 5/8"w grosgrain ribbon, 5/8"w paper-backed fusible web tape, paper-backed fusible web, hot glue gun, five 5/8" dia. buttons, 40" of 1 3/8"w wired ribbon, 10" of floral wire, craft glue, 3" x 5" piece of card stock, 3 1/2" x 5 1/2" piece of corrugated craft cardboard, and a black permanent fine-point marker.

1. Use fabric and follow *Making a Basket Liner*, page 152, to make a liner with fringed edges.
2. Cut four lengths from grosgrain ribbon 1" shorter than each side of liner. Follow manufacturer's instructions to fuse web tape to wrong side of each ribbon length. Overlapping corners as necessary, fuse ribbons to liner inside fringed edges.
3. Use star pattern and follow *Making Appliqués*, page 152, to make five star appliqués from fabric. Fuse one star to liner at each corner. Hot glue one button at center of each star.
4. Use wired ribbon and follow *Making a Bow*, page 153, to make a bow with six 5" loops, a center loop, and two 4" streamers. Use wire to attach bow to handle of basket.
5. For recipe card, use craft glue to glue card stock to cardboard; allow to dry. Fuse remaining star to top left corner of card stock. Hot glue remaining button to center of star. Use marker to draw "stitches" along edges and write serving instructions on recipe card.

This year, give a gift that promises to lift holiday spirits — our Apricot Cream Liqueur! The smooth and creamy cordial is perfect for sipping while relaxing in the comfort of home with friends and family on Christmas Eve. Present the elegant offering in a classy gift bag topped with a bow.

APRICOT CREAM LIQUEUR

2 cups whipping cream

1 can (14 ounces) sweetened condensed milk

1½ cups apricot-flavored brandy

1 can (11½ ounces) apricot nectar

In a 2-quart container, combine whipping cream, sweetened condensed milk, brandy, and apricot nectar. Store in an airtight container in refrigerator. Pour into gift bottles; serve chilled.

Yield: about 7 cups liqueur

LIQUEUR BAG

You will need a black permanent fine-point marker, 5" x 13½" gift bag with handles and matching tag, 24" of 1⅝"w mesh wired ribbon, and 24" of ³/₈"w satin ribbon.

1. Use marker to write message on tag.
2. Place gift in bag. Tie wired ribbon into a bow. Use satin ribbon to attach bow to handles of bag.

CRANBERRY CONFECTIONS

Coated in a winter wonderland of sugary "snow," our Chocolate-Cranberry Balls will bring shouts of Yuletide glee! The sweets are so delicious, your friends will be begging for more. But don't worry — our recipe makes plenty for sharing! For giving, stack the morsels in a festive basket adorned with a pretty poinsettia and bow.

CHOCOLATE-CRANBERRY BALLS

1 cup chocolate graham cracker crumbs (about seven 2¹/₂ x 5-inch crackers)
1 package (6 ounces) sweetened dried cranberries, chopped
2 tablespoons frozen orange juice concentrate, thawed
1 package (6 ounces) semisweet chocolate chips
2 tablespoons butter or margarine
   Confectioners sugar

Pulse process cracker crumbs, cranberries, and orange juice concentrate in a food processor until blended. Combine chocolate chips and butter in a heavy medium saucepan. Stirring constantly, cook over low heat until chocolate melts. Stir in crumb mixture. Cool about 5 minutes or until mixture is cool enough to handle. Shape mixture into 1-inch balls. Roll balls in confectioners sugar and place on waxed paper. Roll in confectioners sugar again, if desired. Store in a single layer between sheets of waxed paper in an airtight container.

Yield: about 3¹/₂ dozen candies

GIFT BASKET AND TAG

You will need 13" of ⁵/₈"w wired ribbon, basket with handle (we used a 4" dia. basket), hot glue gun, 2" dia. artificial poinsettia, black permanent fine-point marker, small purchased gift tag, and 4" of ¹/₁₆"w satin ribbon.

1. Tie wired ribbon into a bow around handle of basket. Glue poinsettia to knot of bow.
2. Use marker to write message on tag. Use satin ribbon to attach tag to poinsettia.

NUTCRACKER SNACKER

A noble nutcracker proudly takes the stage on this gift bag — making it a most distinguished gift. Fill it with our Nutcracker Snack Mix, and your friends will come marching back for more!

NUTCRACKER SNACK MIX

- 8 cups oyster crackers
- 1 jar (12 ounces) dry-roasted peanuts
- 1/2 cup butter or margarine
- 2 packages (0.4 ounce each) ranch-style salad dressing mix

Preheat oven to 300 degrees. In a large roasting pan, combine crackers and peanuts. In a small saucepan, melt butter over medium-low heat. Remove from heat; stir in dressing mix. Pour over cracker mixture; stir until well coated. Bake 20 minutes, stirring every 5 minutes, or until lightly browned. Cool in pan. Store in an airtight container.

Yield: about 10³/₄ cups snack mix

APPLIQUÉD NUTCRACKER BAG

You will need paper-backed fusible web; flesh, black, and assorted fabrics; 12³/₄" of 1¹/₂"w ribbon; 7" x 12" canvas bag with hook and loop fasteners; ¹/₄"w gold metallic braid; fabric glue; one ³/₄" dia. and two ⁵/₈" dia. buttons; black permanent fine-point marker; 1¹/₂" x 2" piece of card stock; hole punch; and small gold cord.

1. Referring to *Making Patterns*, page 152, use patterns, page 143, and follow *Making Appliqués*, page 152, to

make one entire body appliqué, including hat, from flesh fabric; hat, mustache, beard, two eye, and two eyebrow appliqués from black fabric; and remaining appliqués from assorted fabrics. Fuse web to wrong side of ribbon.
2. Overlapping to bottom, fuse ribbon ¹/₈" from left edge on front of bag. Fuse body to front of bag. Overlapping as necessary, arrange and fuse remaining appliqués on body.

3. Cut one 2¹/₂" and two 1" pieces of braid. Glue 2¹/₂" piece of braid to plume on hat and two 1" pieces of braid on shoulders; allow to dry. Glue ³/₄" dia. button at top of ribbon strip; glue ⁵/₈" dia. buttons on coat. Allow to dry.
4. Place gift in bag.
5. For tag, use marker to draw border along edges and write message on card stock. Punch a hole in corner of tag. Use cord to attach tag to ³/₄" dia. button.

FOR FUDGE FANS

*F*udge fans won't be able to keep their mittens off our Chocolate-Coconut Cream Fudge when you deliver it in a wintry appliquéd box! Chock-full of rich flavor, the old-fashioned candy will melt in their mouths.

CHOCOLATE-COCONUT CREAM FUDGE

2¼ cups sugar
1 can (8½ ounces) cream of coconut
1 cup evaporated milk
2 tablespoons light corn syrup
1 tablespoon butter or margarine
⅛ teaspoon salt
1 teaspoon vanilla extract
1 package (6 ounces) semisweet chocolate chips

Line a 9-inch square baking pan with aluminum foil, extending foil over 2 sides of pan; grease foil. Butter sides of a heavy large saucepan. Combine sugar, cream of coconut, evaporated milk, corn syrup, butter, and salt. Stirring constantly, cook over medium-low heat until sugar dissolves. Using a pastry brush dipped in hot water, wash down any sugar crystals on sides of pan. Attach a candy thermometer to pan, making sure thermometer does not touch bottom of pan. Increase heat to medium and bring to a boil. Cook, without stirring, until mixture reaches soft-ball stage (approximately 234 to 240 degrees). Test about ½ teaspoon mixture in ice water. Mixture will easily form a ball in ice water but will flatten when removed from water. Place pan in 2 inches of cold water in sink. Add vanilla; do not stir. Cool to

approximately 110 degrees. Remove from sink. Stir in chocolate chips. Using medium speed of an electric mixer, beat until fudge thickens and begins to lose its gloss. Pour into prepared pan. Chill 1 hour or until firm.

Use ends of foil to lift fudge from pan. Cut into 1-inch squares. Store in an airtight container in refrigerator.

Yield: about 5½ dozen pieces fudge

MITTEN BOX

You will need a mitten-shaped papier-mâché box with lid, paper-backed fusible web, fabrics for mitten and heart, fleece for cuff, and a hot glue gun.

1. Using box lid as a pattern and heart pattern, page 135, follow *Making Appliqués*, page 152, to make one mitten and one heart appliqué from fabrics.
2. Fuse mitten appliqué to box lid; center and fuse heart appliqué on mitten appliqué.
3. For cuff, measure width of mitten at "wrist." Cut a piece from fleece 1"w by the determined measurement. Glue cuff along "wrist" edge of mitten appliqué.

CHRISTMAS CONFETTI

*S*pread some holiday zest with our fun and fruity Confetti Salsa! Made from a blend of citrus fruit, peppers, and more, this tangy treat will be a hit at holiday parties. Top a jar of the salsa with fabric, ribbon, and faux holly sprigs; then pack in a lined basket along with tortilla chips. For a finishing touch, glue a Christmas card cutout to the front of the basket.

CONFETTI SALSA

- 2 limes
- 2 oranges
- 1 cup chopped jícama
- 1 cup chopped sweet red pepper
- 1 cup chopped red onion
- 2 tablespoons chopped fresh mint leaves
- 2 tablespoons olive oil
- 1 tablespoon seeded and chopped jalapeño pepper
- 1 tablespoon drained capers
- 1 tablespoon white balsamic vinegar
- 1 teaspoon salt
   Tortilla chips to serve

Grate 1 teaspoon zest *each* from a lime and an orange. Peel and section pulp from limes and oranges; chop into 1/2-inch pieces. In a medium bowl, combine lime and orange sections, jícama, red pepper, onion, mint, oil, jalapeño pepper, capers, vinegar, lime zest, orange zest, and salt. Stir until well blended. Cover and store in refrigerator 2 hours to let flavors blend. Serve with tortilla chips.

Yield: about 3 1/2 cups salsa

CHRISTMAS CARD BASKET

You will need fabric for liner and jar lid cover, basket with handle (we used an 8" x 11" basket), hot glue gun, 3/4"w red grosgrain ribbon, Christmas card, card stock to coordinate with Christmas card, three artificial holly sprigs with berries, jar with lid, pinking shears, and a rubber band.

1. Use fabric for liner and follow *Making a Basket Liner*, page 152, to make a liner with unfinished edges.
2. Trimming to fit and gluing each end, wrap ribbon around handle of basket.
3. Cut design from card. Glue design to card stock. Leaving a 1/4" card stock border, cut out card. Arrange and glue two holly sprigs, then card to front of basket.
4. For jar lid cover, draw around jar lid on wrong side of fabric. Use pinking shears to cut out circle 2 1/2" outside drawn line. Center circle over lid; secure with rubber band. Measure around lid; add 18". Cut a length of ribbon the determined measurement. Tie ribbon into a bow around lid, covering rubber band. Glue remaining holly sprig to knot of bow.
5. Place liner and jar in basket.

PEPPERMINT PERFECTION

*F*or an irresistible taste sensation, combine peppermint and white chocolate to create a delightfully sweet treat. For a perfect presentation, deliver the minty confections in a gift bag cleverly disguised as an elf.

PEPPERMINT SWIRL BUTTER

- 11 ounces white candy coating, chopped and divided
- 6 ounces white baking chocolate, chopped
- 1/4 cup finely ground peppermint candies
- 1 tablespoon whipping cream
- 1/4 teaspoon red paste food coloring

Line a 10¹/₂ x 15¹/₂-inch jellyroll pan with aluminum foil, extending foil over ends of pan; grease foil. In a medium saucepan, combine 10 ounces candy coating and chocolate. Stirring constantly, melt over low heat. Remove from heat; leave in warm saucepan. Combine candies and whipping cream in a small saucepan. Stirring constantly, melt over low heat. Stir in food coloring. Add remaining 1 ounce candy coating to peppermint mixture; stir until smooth. Spread untinted chocolate into prepared pan; drizzle with peppermint mixture. Use tip of a knife to swirl peppermint mixture into chocolate. Firmly rap bottom of pan against counter to smooth surface of mixture. Chill 1 hour or until candy hardens.

Break into pieces. Store in an airtight container in refrigerator.

Yield: about 1 pound candy

ELF BAG

You will need a 7" x 10" gift bag, fabric, hot glue gun, 25" of ¹/₄"w black ribbon, tracing paper, poster board, transfer paper, red colored pencil, red and black permanent fine-point markers, toddler-size sock, and a craft glue stick.

1. Fold top of bag 2¹/₂" to front; unfold. Cutting to within ³/₄" of fold, cut a sawtooth design across top of bag. Refold bag.
2. Tear two 2" x 10" strips for arms and two 2" x 15" strips for legs from fabric. Tie knots in arms for "wrists" and "elbows." Tie knots in legs for "ankles" and "knees." Hot glue arms to sides of bag and legs to bottom of bag. Tie ribbon into a knot around bag for belt; hot glue to secure.
3. Trace head pattern, page 131, onto tracing paper; cut out. Draw around pattern on poster board; cut out. Use transfer paper to transfer face to head. Use red pencil to add cheeks and highlights to ears. Use black marker to draw over eyes, eyebrows, and nose. Use red marker to draw over mouth.
4. Hot glue head to back of bag. For cap, fold cuff of sock 1" to right side twice. Hot glue cap to top of head.
5. Unfold bag and place gift in bag; refold and use glue stick to glue fold in place.

BLUEBERRY BREAKFAST

*B*righten a friend's morning with our quick-to-fix Lemon-Oatmeal Pancake Mix. She'll appreciate how easy it is to whip up, and the Blueberry Syrup will top off everything deliciously! Make her feel special by snuggling the mix and syrup in a hand-decorated heart basket. And for the finale, include an apron adorned with a gingerbread man and holiday hearts.

BLUEBERRY SYRUP

- 1 package (12 ounces) frozen blueberries
- 2 cups water
- 1 cup light corn syrup
- 1 package (1³/₄ ounces) powdered fruit pectin
- 4 cups sugar

In a Dutch oven, combine blueberries, water, corn syrup, and pectin over medium-high heat. Stirring constantly, bring to a rolling boil. Add sugar. Stirring constantly, bring to a rolling boil again and boil 1 minute. Remove from heat. Pour into heat-resistant jars; cover and cool to room temperature. Store in refrigerator. Serve with Lemon-Oatmeal Pancakes.

Yield: about 5¹/₂ cups syrup

LEMON-OATMEAL PANCAKE MIX

Make several batches of mix to give with Blueberry Syrup.

- 2 cups all-purpose baking mix
- ¹/₂ cup nonfat milk powder
- ¹/₂ cup quick-cooking oats
- 2 tablespoons sugar
- 2 teaspoons grated lemon zest

In a large bowl, combine baking mix, milk powder, oats, sugar, and lemon zest. Store in an airtight container in refrigerator. Give with serving instructions.

Yield: about 3 cups mix

To serve: In a medium bowl, combine 3 cups pancake mix, 1³/₄ cups water, and 2 slightly beaten eggs. Stir just until moistened. Heat a greased griddle over medium heat. For each pancake, pour about ¹/₄ cup batter onto griddle and cook until top of pancake is full of bubbles and underside is golden brown. Turn with a spatula and cook until remaining side is golden brown. Grease griddle as necessary. Serve warm with Blueberry Syrup.

Yield: about 14 pancakes

GINGERBREAD BASKET AND APRON

BASKET AND BAGS
You will need ecru and red acrylic paint, paintbrushes, three 2¹/₈" x 4¹/₈" unfinished wooden hearts, hot glue gun, basket (we used a 7³/₄" x 11¹/₄" basket with handle), black permanent fine-point marker, two 2¹/₄" x 3" pieces of white card stock, craft glue stick, two brown lunch-size paper bags, hole punch, several 20" lengths of raffia, and shredded paper.

Allow paint to dry after each application.

1. Paint each heart red. Use end of paintbrush to paint ecru dots on hearts. Arrange and hot glue hearts on one side of basket.
2. For each label, use marker to write contents of bag and draw border on card stock piece.

3. For each bag, center and use glue stick to glue label on bag. Place gift in bag. Fold top of bag 1¹/₂" to front. Punch two holes ³/₄" apart in center folded portion of bag. Thread several lengths of raffia through holes in bag; tie into a bow at front of bag.
4. Fill basket with shredded paper. Place bags in basket.

APRON
You will need paper-backed fusible web; red and brown fabrics; adult-size canvas apron; ecru, pink, and black acrylic paint; paintbrushes; white dimensional paint; black permanent fine-point marker; 5" of ¹/₈"w ribbon; hot glue gun; and three ¹/₄" dia. buttons.

Allow paint to dry after each application.

1. Use patterns, page 138, and follow *Making Appliqués*, page 152, to make one gingerbread man appliqué from brown fabric and two heart appliqués from red fabric. Arrange and fuse appliqués on apron.
2. Use acrylic paint to paint face on gingerbread man. Use dimensional paint to add details to gingerbread man. Use end of paintbrush to paint ecru dots on hearts. Use marker to outline gingerbread man and hearts.
3. Tie ribbon into a bow. Glue bow and buttons to gingerbread man.

BLISSFUL BREAD

*E*veryone knows that homemade bread is best, but ours tops the list! Chocolate, bananas, and walnuts swirled together make this dessert a tasty temptation. For a personal touch, deliver the treat in a hand-painted basket lined with a decorative napkin.

CHOCOLATE SWIRL BANANA BREAD

- 1/2 cup vegetable shortening
- 1/2 cup granulated sugar
- 1/2 cup firmly packed brown sugar
- 2 eggs
- 1 1/2 cups mashed bananas (about 3 bananas)
- 1 teaspoon vanilla extract
- 2 cups all-purpose flour
- 1 teaspoon baking soda
- 1 teaspoon salt
- 2 ounces semisweet baking chocolate, melted
- 1 cup chopped walnuts, toasted

Preheat oven to 325 degrees. Grease two 3 3/4 x 7 1/2-inch loaf pans. Line bottoms of pans with waxed paper; grease waxed paper. In a large bowl, cream shortening and sugars until fluffy. Add eggs, 1 at a time, beating well after each addition. Add bananas and vanilla; beat just until blended. In a small bowl, combine flour, baking soda, and salt. Add dry ingredients to creamed mixture; stir until well blended. Remove 3/4 cup batter and place in a small bowl; stir in melted chocolate. Stir walnuts into remaining plain batter. Spoon nut batter into prepared pans. Drop chocolate batter by tablespoonfuls over nut batter. Swirl batters with a knife. Bake 58 to 62 minutes

or until a toothpick inserted in center of bread comes out clean. Cool in pans on a wire rack 10 minutes. Remove from pans and cool completely on a wire rack. Store in an airtight container.

Yield: 2 loaves bread

PAINTED BASKET

You will need red and green acrylic paint, paintbrushes, 5" x 11 1/2" basket with handles, toothbrush, paper towel, colored pencils, photocopy of tag design (page 149) on white card stock, black permanent fine-point marker, decorative-edge craft scissors, hole punch, 24" of 1/4"w satin ribbon, and a decorative fabric napkin for basket liner.

Allow paint to dry after each application.

1. Paint green stripes on handles and green squares around rim of basket. Use red paint to outline squares and paint wavy lines and dots around rim. Follow *Spatter Painting*, page 153, to spatter paint basket green.

2. Use colored pencils to color tag. Use marker to write message on tag. Use craft scissors to cut out tag 1/4" outside outer lines. Punch hole in corner of tag. Use ribbon to attach tag to basket.

3. Line basket with napkin, then place gift in basket.

MERRY MUSHROOMS TO YOU

*O*ur Mushroom Cheese Spread
will make anyone's Christmas a
bit zestier! It's a rich blend of
mushrooms, zippy seasonings, and
two kinds of cheese — a true palate
pleaser! Package the gift in a festive
appliquéd wreath bag and include
some crackers for serving.

MUSHROOM CHEESE SPREAD

- 1 package (8 ounces) fresh
    mushrooms, coarsely chopped
- 1/2 cup Italian salad dressing
- 2 packages (8 ounces each) cream
    cheese, softened
- 2 cups (8 ounces) shredded
    Monterey Jack cheese
- 1/4 cup finely chopped green onions
    Chopped green onion to garnish
    Crackers to serve

In a medium skillet, sauté mushrooms
in salad dressing over medium heat until
most of liquid evaporates. Remove from
heat; set aside.

In a large bowl, beat cream cheese
until fluffy. Beat in Monterey Jack cheese
until well blended. Stir in mushrooms and
1/4 cup green onions. Spoon into serving
containers. Garnish with additional green
onion. Cover and store in refrigerator.
Serve with crackers.

Yield: about 4 cups spread

APPLIQUÉD WREATH BAG

You will need paper-backed fusible web;
assorted red and green fabrics; white gift
bag; one 18" length each of 1/4"w satin
ribbon, 1/2"w gold wired ribbon, and 1/8"
dia. gold cord; hot glue gun; and tissue
paper.

1. Use patterns, page 136, and follow
Making Appliqués, page 152, to make
36 leaf appliqués from green fabrics and
eight berry appliqués from red fabrics.
Measure width of bag; make two strip
appliqués 1/2"w by the determined
measurement from green fabrics.
2. Fuse strips along top and bottom edges
on front of bag. Arrange leaf and berry

appliqués into a wreath shape on front of
bag; fuse in place.
3. Tie ribbons and cord together into a
bow. Knot ends of ribbons and cord. Glue
bow to wreath.
4. Line bag with tissue paper. Place gift
in bag.

A "BERRY" MERRY TREAT

*W*arm their hearts with this vanilla-berry beverage! Given in a handcrafted snowman bag, our cocoa mix is flavored with a hint of vanilla and raspberry. It's a fun Yuletide gift for that special little girl or boy. But don't forget the "big" kids — they'll love the yummy mix as well!

VANILLA-BERRY COCOA MIX

6   cups nonfat milk powder
2   jars (8 ounces each) French vanilla-flavored non-dairy powdered creamer
1   package (16 ounces) confectioners sugar
1   package (15 ounces) chocolate mix for milk
1   package (0.15 ounce) unsweetened raspberry-flavored soft drink mix
1/2   teaspoon salt

In a very large bowl, combine milk powder, creamer, confectioners sugar, chocolate mix, soft drink mix, and salt. Store in an airtight container in a cool place. Give with serving instructions.

Yield: about 13 cups cocoa mix

To serve: Pour 6 ounces hot water over about 2 1/2 heaping tablespoons cocoa mix; stir until well blended.

SNOWMAN BAG

You will need yellow, orange and black acrylic paint; paintbrushes; 4 1/4" x 8" white gift bag; hot glue gun; 1" x 6" strip of black craft foam; fabric; tracing paper; transfer paper; black permanent fine-point marker; two 5/8" dia. black buttons for eyes; and an artificial holly sprig.

1. For hat, paint top 2 3/4" of bag black; allow to dry. Center and glue foam strip along bottom edge of hat.
2. Tear one 1 1/2" x 8" strip for streamers and one 1 1/2" x 26" strip for scarf from fabric. Overlapping ends at back, glue scarf around bottom of bag. Tie a knot in center of streamers; fringe ends. Glue knot in streamers to scarf.

3. Trace pattern, page 136, onto tracing paper. Use transfer paper to transfer nose and mouth to front of bag. Paint nose orange with yellow highlights; allow to dry. Use marker to draw over mouth and add detail lines on nose. Glue eyes to bag. Glue holly sprig to hat.
4. Place gift in bag. Fold top of bag 1/2" to back; glue to secure.

TASTE BUD "TEA-SER"

Brew away the winter chills with a hot cup of tea made with our Apricot-Mint Tea Mix! Friends will enjoy relaxing by the fire while sipping the delightful blend. For an appealing presentation, pack a bag of the mix in a basket along with some hand-painted snowman coasters.

APRICOT-MINT TEA MIX

- 2 cups unsweetened powdered instant tea
- 2 packages (3 ounces each) apricot gelatin
- 1¹⁄₂ cups sugar
- ¹⁄₂ teaspoon peppermint extract

Process ingredients in a food processor until well blended. Store in an airtight container. Give with serving instructions.

Yield: about 2²⁄₃ cups tea mix

To serve: Pour 6 ounces hot water over 1 level tablespoon tea mix; stir until well blended.

PAINTED COASTERS AND BAG

For bag and four coasters, you will need white, red, blue, green, and black acrylic paint; assorted paintbrushes; four 3¹⁄₂" dia. white ceramic coasters; tracing paper; transfer paper; black permanent fine-point marker; toothbrush; paper towel; foam paintbrush; clear acrylic sealer; 9" x 10" piece of checked flannel fabric; several 20" lengths of red raffia; 7" x 8¹⁄₂" basket; and natural excelsior.

Allow glue, paint, and sealer to dry after each application.

1. For each coaster, paint top and sides of coaster blue. Trace pattern, page 135, onto tracing paper. Use transfer paper to transfer snowman to center of coaster. Referring to pattern for color placement, paint snowman. Use marker to outline and add details to snowman. Paint a red and green striped border around edges and on sides of coaster. Use liner brush to paint white "snowflakes" around snowman and highlight boots.

2. Follow *Spatter Painting*, page 153, to spatter paint coasters white. Use foam brush to apply two to three coats of sealer to top and sides of coaster.

3. Use fabric and follow *Making a Fabric Bag*, page 154, to make a bag.

4. Place gift in bag. Tie raffia into a bow around top of bag.

5. Line basket with excelsior. Place bag and coasters in basket.

JALAPEÑO HOTTIE

*W*ho wants to eat ice cream that's hot? Everyone will, once they try our Hot Hot Fudge Sauce! We've added spicy jalapeño flavor to everyone's favorite ice-cream topping to make it simply scrumptious! But it's not just good on ice cream — it's also yummy served warm over cake. Deliver the fabulous fudge sauce in a cute snow lady bag.

HOT HOT FUDGE SAUCE

- 1   cup sugar
- 1   cup light corn syrup
- 1/2   cup cocoa
- 1/2   cup evaporated milk
- 3   tablespoons butter or margarine
- 1/4   teaspoon salt
- 1   teaspoon vanilla extract
- 1   to 2 tablespoons seeded and minced jalapeño pepper

In a medium saucepan, combine sugar, corn syrup, cocoa, evaporated milk, butter, and salt. Stirring constantly, cook over medium heat until sugar dissolves and mixture is smooth (about 7 minutes). Remove from heat; stir in vanilla and jalapeño pepper. Serve warm or at room temperature over ice cream or cake. Store in an airtight container in refrigerator.

Yield: about 2²/₃ cups sauce

SNOW LADY BAG

You will need white, orange, pink, and red felt; tracing paper; drawing compass; hot glue gun; two 1/2" dia. black buttons for eyes; black embroidery floss; rubber band; and 16" of 1¹/₂"w satin ribbon.

Refer to Embroidery Stitches, page 152, before beginning project.

1. Cut an 8" x 24" piece from white felt. Use felt piece and follow *Making a Fabric Bag*, page 154, to make a bag.
2. Trace nose and mouth patterns, page 133, onto tracing paper; cut out. Using patterns, cut nose from orange felt and mouth from red felt. For cheeks, use compass to draw two 1" dia. circles on pink felt; cut out.

3. Glue eyes, nose, mouth, and cheeks on bag. Using six strands of floss, work *Straight Stitches* for eyelashes and *Running Stitches* for mouth.
4. For hair, make 1¹/₂" long cuts at 1/4" intervals across top of bag. Place gift in bag. Gather top of bag; secure with rubber band. Fold hair down, covering rubber band.
5. Tie ribbon into a bow. Glue bow at top of bag.

CINNAMON SWIRL

A swirl of sugar, cinnamon, and toasted pecans makes this bread a tasty breakfast treat! Our Cinnamon Roll Bread would make a splendid gift for that special friend or co-worker who brightens your life throughout the year. Present the flavorful gift (along with your warmest wishes) in an appliquéd canvas bag.

CINNAMON ROLL BREAD

- 1 loaf (16 ounces) frozen white yeast dough, thawed in refrigerator overnight
- 1/2 cup butter or margarine, softened
- 1/2 cup granulated sugar
- 1/4 cup chopped pecans, toasted
- 2 teaspoons ground cinnamon
  Vegetable oil cooking spray
- 1 cup confectioners sugar
- 1 1/2 tablespoons milk
- 1/2 teaspoon vanilla extract

Let dough stand at room temperature 30 minutes. On a lightly floured surface, use a floured rolling pin to roll dough into a 10 x 12-inch rectangle. Spread butter over dough. In a small bowl, combine granulated sugar, pecans, and cinnamon. Sprinkle sugar mixture over butter to within 1 inch of edges. Beginning at 1 short edge, roll up dough jellyroll style. Pinch seam to seal. Place, seam side down, in a greased 4 1/2 x 8 1/2-inch loaf pan, turning ends under. Spray top of dough with cooking spray, cover, and let rise in a warm place (80 to 85 degrees) about 30 minutes or until almost doubled in size.

Preheat oven to 350 degrees. Cut 5 slashes in top of loaf. Bake 30 to 35 minutes or until golden brown. Cool in pan 5 minutes. Transfer to a wire rack with waxed paper underneath. In a small bowl, combine confectioners sugar, milk, and vanilla; stir until smooth. Drizzle icing over warm loaf. Serve warm or cool completely. Store in an airtight container.

Yield: 1 loaf bread

CANVAS MITTEN BAG

You will need paper-backed fusible web, assorted fabrics for appliqués, canvas bag (we used a 10" x 5" x 4 1/2" bag with handles), hot glue gun, two 5/8" dia. buttons for each pair of mittens, black permanent fine-point marker, and tissue paper.

1. For each pair of mittens, use pattern, page 136, and follow *Making Appliqués*, page 152, to make two (one in reverse) mitten appliqués from fabrics.
2. Arrange and fuse mittens on bag. Glue one button at outer corner of each mitten at wrist. Use marker to draw a squiggly line to connect mittens.
3. Line bag with tissue paper. Place gift in bag.

CHRISTMAS AT THE RANCH

*F*or *a quick and zesty treat, whip up a batch of our Instant Ranch Potato Soup for a mom on the run. Complete the hearty gift with crunchy Ranch Cheese Crackers — a fitting complement for a sumptuous soup! Pack the savory mix in a stamped gift bag — and be sure to include a hand-decorated mug for a heartwarming touch.*

INSTANT RANCH POTATO SOUP

- 4 cups potato flakes
- 2 cups nonfat milk powder
- 1/4 cup chicken bouillon granules
- 1 package (0.4 ounce) ranch-style salad dressing mix
- 1 teaspoon garlic powder
- 1/2 teaspoon ground black pepper

Combine all ingredients in a large bowl; stir until well blended. Store in an airtight container. Give with serving instructions.

Yield: about 6 1/4 cups of mix

To serve: Place 1/2 cup soup mix in a soup bowl or mug. Add 1 cup boiling water and stir until smooth. Let soup stand 1 to 2 minutes to thicken slightly.

RANCH CHEESE CRACKERS

- 4 dozen cheese-flavored saltine crackers
- 1/4 cup butter or margarine
- 1 package (0.4 ounce) ranch-style salad dressing mix

Preheat oven to 325 degrees. Place crackers in a single layer in two 10 1/2 x 15 1/2-inch jellyroll pans. In a small saucepan, melt butter over medium heat. Remove from heat; stir in salad dressing mix. Brush butter mixture over crackers. Bake 6 to 8 minutes or until lightly browned. Cool crackers in pans. Store in an airtight container.

Yield: 4 dozen crackers

STAMPED BAG AND MUG

You will need a white gift bag with handles, ruler, cutting mat, craft knife, tree-motif rubber stamp, green ink pad, gold acrylic paint, liner paintbrush, 1 1/2"w wired ribbon, white card stock, hot glue gun, Create-A-Mug™, decorative-edge craft scissors, red permanent fine-point marker, and tissue paper.

Allow ink and paint to dry after each application.

1. Beginning 1" below top of bag, use ruler to mark an even number of 1 3/4" long vertical lines 1" apart across front of bag. Cutting through front of bag only, use craft knife to cut lines.

2. Stamp trees on front of bag. Paint small gold stars at top of each tree; use end of paintbrush to paint gold dots on trees.

3. Measure around bag; add 20". Cut a length of ribbon the determined measurement. Starting with center of ribbon at center back of bag, wrap ribbon around bag to front; weave ribbon ends through cut lines and tie into a bow.

4. For mug insert, cut a 3 5/8" x 11" piece from card stock. Cut two 11" lengths of ribbon. Matching long edges and wrong sides, press ribbon lengths in half. Place long edges of card stock between folds of ribbons; glue to secure. Follow Step 2 to stamp and paint trees along center of card stock. Follow manufacturer's instructions to place insert in mug and to wash mug.

5. For tag, use craft scissors to cut a 3" x 5" piece from card stock. Use marker to draw dots and dashes along edges of tag. Follow Step 2 to stamp and paint one tree on left side of tag. Use marker to write serving instructions on tag. Spot glue tag to bag.

6. Line bag with tissue paper. Place gift and mug in bag.

Place 1/2 cup
mix in a soup
or mug. Add
boiling water
stir until smoo...
soup stand 1 t...
minutes to thi...
slightly.

41

PENGUIN PARTY

For a gift that's full of cheer, give our yummy Penguin Treats! These tasty mouthfuls are chock-full of chocolate and butterscotch chips — a delicious combination! Garnished with pecan halves, the chewy cookies are even more delightful when carried in a perky penguin gift bag.

PENGUIN TREATS

1 can (14 ounces) sweetened condensed milk
1 package (6 ounces) semisweet chocolate chips
1 cup butterscotch chips
$1/4$ cup butter or margarine
1 teaspoon vanilla extract
$1^1/_2$ cups all-purpose flour
$3/_4$ cup small pecan halves

Preheat oven to 350 degrees. Line a baking sheet with parchment paper. In top of a double boiler, combine sweetened condensed milk, chocolate chips, butterscotch chips, and butter. Stirring constantly, cook over simmering water until mixture is smooth. Remove from heat; add vanilla. Stir in flour. Drop by teaspoonfuls onto prepared baking sheet. Press a pecan half into center of each cookie. Bake 7 to 9 minutes (do not overbake). Cool cookies on baking sheet 2 minutes; transfer to a wire rack to cool completely. Store in an airtight container.

Yield: about 9 dozen cookies

PENGUIN BAG

You will need tracing paper; white, yellow, and black card stock; yellow and gold acrylic paint; flat paintbrush; $5^1/_2$"w

wooden heart; hot glue gun; black lunch-size gift bag; 15" of $1^1/_2$"w ribbon; two $3/_4$" long oval-shaped wiggle eyes; and a black permanent fine-point marker.

1. Trace patterns, page 137, onto tracing paper; cut out. Draw around patterns and cut one beak from yellow card stock, one body from white card stock, and two wings from black card stock.

2. Paint wooden heart gold for feet; allow to dry. To outline body, slightly dampen paintbrush, then dip one side of paintbrush in yellow paint. With paint side of paintbrush along outer edges of body, pull paintbrush along body outline. Allow to dry.

3. Arrange and glue body to front of bag. Glue feet to bottom of bag. Fold straight edge of wings $1/2$" to back. Arrange and glue wings on side of bag even with front of bag.

4. Tie ribbon into a bow. Arrange and glue bow, eyes, and beak on body. Use marker to draw eyelashes.

5. Place gift in bag. Fold corners of bag to back; glue to secure.

MORNING MUFFINS

*M*oist and flavorful, our *Pumpkin-Chocolate Chip Muffins* are a perfect treat to eat while opening presents on Christmas morning! The mouth-watering muffins would also make a wonderful gift to share with co-workers. Carry the homemade goodies in a beribboned basket lined with festive star-appliquéd felt.

PUMPKIN-CHOCOLATE CHIP MUFFINS

  1 cup canned pumpkin
  2 eggs
  1 cup firmly packed brown sugar
  1/4 cup vegetable oil
  3 cups all-purpose baking mix
  1 teaspoon pumpkin pie spice
  1 package (6 ounces) semisweet chocolate chips
  3/4 cup chopped pecans, toasted

Preheat oven to 400 degrees. Line a muffin pan with paper muffin cups. In a large bowl, combine pumpkin, eggs, brown sugar, and oil. Add baking mix and spice; beat just until blended. Stir in chocolate chips and pecans. Fill muffin cups about two-thirds full. Bake 14 to 18 minutes until golden brown or until a toothpick inserted in center of muffin comes out clean. Serve warm or cool on a wire rack. Store in an airtight container.

Yield: about 1 1/2 dozen muffins

STAR BASKET LINER

You will need ecru felt, paper-backed fusible web, yellow fabric, green embroidery floss, glossy wood-tone spray, basket (we used a 7" x 10 1/2" basket), 1 1/2"w wired ribbon, hot glue gun, and an artificial holly and berry sprig.

1. For liner, cut a 7" x 20" piece from felt. Refer to Fig. 1 to cut off corners of liner at each end.

Fig. 1

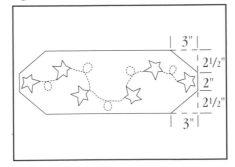

2. Use pattern, page 131, and follow *Making Appliqués,* page 152, to make six star appliqués from fabric. Refer to Fig. 1 to arrange stars on liner; fuse in place.
3. Using six strands of floss, work *Running Stitches,* page 152, along edges of liner and around each star; work a "squiggly" line to connect stars.
4. Lightly apply wood-tone spray to basket; allow to dry.
5. Measure around rim of basket; add 21". Cut a length of ribbon the determined measurement. Tie ribbon into a bow around basket. Glue holly sprig at center of bow.
6. Place liner and gift in basket.

LAVISHLY LEMON

There's no doubt about it, our Luscious Lemon Meringue Pie will be loved by all! The lavish pie boasts a temptingly sweet lemon filling topped off with a smooth and sumptuous meringue. Present the delectable delight in a wire basket embellished with a white poinsettia, ivy, and delicate pearls.

LUSCIOUS LEMON MERINGUE PIE

FILLING

- 1²/₃ cups sugar
- ¹/₂ cup cornstarch
- ¹/₄ teaspoon salt
- 1³/₄ cups water
- ¹/₂ cup freshly squeezed lemon juice
- 4 egg yolks, beaten
- 3 tablespoons butter or margarine
- 1 tablespoon grated lemon zest
- 1 baked 9-inch pie crust

MERINGUE

- 4 egg whites
- ¹/₂ teaspoon cream of tartar
- ¹/₈ teaspoon salt
- ³/₄ cup confectioners sugar
- ¹/₂ teaspoon lemon extract

For filling, combine sugar, cornstarch, salt, water, lemon juice, and egg yolks in a heavy large saucepan. Stirring constantly, cook over medium heat until mixture boils and thickens. Continue stirring and boil 1 minute. Remove from heat; stir in butter and lemon zest. Spoon into pie crust.

Preheat oven to 350 degrees. For meringue, beat egg whites, cream of tartar, and salt in a large bowl until foamy.

Gradually add confectioners sugar, beating until stiff peaks form. Beat in lemon extract. Spread meringue over hot filling, sealing to edge of crust. Bake 12 to 14 minutes or until meringue is golden brown. Cool on a wire rack. Store in an airtight container in refrigerator.

Yield: about 8 servings

WIRE PIE CARRIER

You will need 1 yd. of 2"w satin-edged sheer white ribbon, craft wire, wire cutters, one artificial white poinsettia cut from stem, artificial gold and green ivy pick, pearl stem, pie basket with handle (we used a 10¹/₂" dia. metal basket), self-adhesive gift tag, gold card stock, hole punch, and a 6" length of gold cord.

1. Use ribbon and follow *Making a Bow*, page 153, to make a bow with four 6" loops and two 5" streamers. Wire bow, poinsettia, ivy, and pearl stem to handle of basket.
2. Apply gift tag to card stock. Trim card stock to ¹/₈" from edges of tag. Punch hole in corner of tag. Thread cord through hole in tag and knot cord ends together. Hang tag on pearl stem.
3. Place gift in basket.

PERFECTLY PEACHY

*F**or a perfectly peachy gift,
give some of our Peach-Flavored
Vinegar! The tangy topper adds a
splash of flavor to salads and is
also great served with meats. The
condiment can even be mixed with
a few other pantry staples to create
Peachy Salad Dressing. For an eye-
catching presentation, pour the
vinegar in a decorative bottle tied
with ribbons; then nestle in a lined
basket. Be sure and include the
salad dressing recipe for a
thoughtful touch.*

PEACH-FLAVORED VINEGAR

1 can (15¼ ounces) sliced peaches
    in heavy syrup, undrained
4 cups white vinegar
1 can (12½ ounces) peach nectar
¼ cup sugar
1 whole nutmeg, crushed

In a 2-quart nonmetal bowl, crush
peaches. Add vinegar, peach nectar, sugar,
and nutmeg. Cover and store in a cool
place 3 days to let flavors blend.

Strain vinegar into gift bottles. Store
in refrigerator up to 1 month. Give with
recipe for Peachy Salad Dressing.

Yield: about 6 cups flavored vinegar

PEACHY SALAD DRESSING

½ cup Peach-Flavored Vinegar
¼ cup vegetable oil
½ teaspoon salt
¼ teaspoon paprika
⅛ teaspoon ground black pepper

In a small bowl, combine vinegar, oil,
salt, paprika, and pepper; whisk until well
blended. Store in an airtight container in
refrigerator. Serve with salad greens.

Yield: about ¾ cup dressing

PEACHY BASKET

You will need 30" each of ⅝"w grosgrain
ribbon and two coordinating colors of
¼"w satin ribbon, bottle with stopper to
fit in basket, black fine-point permanent
marker, decorative note paper, fabric, and
a basket (we used a 7½" dia. x 6" tall
basket with handle).

1. Tie ribbons together into a bow around
neck of bottle.
2. Use marker to write Peachy Salad
Dressing recipe on note paper.
3. Use fabric for liner and follow *Making
a Basket Liner*, page 152, to make a liner
with finished edges.
4. Place liner, bottle, and recipe in basket.

FRUIT DIP IN A FLASH

*P*repared *in minutes, this
creamy concoction is a delicious
way to sweeten a holiday get-together!
Our Easy Fruit Dip will be such a hit
among party guests, they won't want
to leave. Make a dazzling display by
placing the dip in a sparkling silver
basket and liner accented with sheer
silver ribbon and pearls.*

EASY FRUIT DIP

   1 package (8 ounces) cream cheese,
          softened
   1 jar (7 ounces) marshmallow creme
 1/4 teaspoon ground ginger
 1/4 cup orange marmalade
       Fresh fruit to serve

In a medium bowl, beat cream cheese
until fluffy. Beat in marshmallow creme
and ginger. Fold in orange marmalade.
Store in an airtight container in
refrigerator. Serve with fresh fruit.

Yield: about 2 cups fruit dip

LINED SILVER BASKET

You will need a 24" square piece of silver
fabric, basket (we used a 7¹/₂" x 9³/₄"
silver metal basket), 24" of 2¹/₂"w silver
sheer wired ribbon, hot glue gun, and a
pearl pick.

1. Use fabric and follow *Making a Basket
Liner*, page 152, to make a liner with
finished edges.
2. Tie ribbon into a bow. Glue pick and
bow to basket.
3. Place liner and gift in basket.

TASTY TOPPING

A snap to make, our Lemon Yogurt Salad Dressing will treat any salad to a tart and tangy topping! Fill a jar with this zesty dressing and add an elegant topper adorned with ribbon and gold baubles; then cradle the jar in a spray-painted basket lined with gold excelsior.

LEMON YOGURT SALAD DRESSING

  1 container (8 ounces) lemon yogurt
  3 tablespoons vegetable oil
  1 tablespoon apple cider vinegar
  $1/2$ teaspoon ground cumin
  $1/2$ teaspoon ground ginger
  $1/2$ teaspoon salt
  $1/4$ teaspoon ground black pepper

In a small bowl, combine yogurt, oil, vinegar, cumin, ginger, salt, and pepper; stir until well blended. Store in an airtight container in refrigerator. Serve with salad greens.

Yield: about 1 cup dressing

BASKET AND JAR LID TOPPER

You will need gold and green spray paint, basket (we used a $5^1/2$" square basket with handle), half-pint jar with lid, ecru handmade paper, rubber band, 2"w wired ribbon, hot glue gun, gold ball floral pick, and gold excelsior.

1. Spray paint basket green; allow to dry. Lightly spray paint basket gold; allow to dry.
2. For jar lid cover, draw around lid on paper; cut out circle 2" outside drawn line. Center circle over lid. Gather edges of circle around sides of lid; secure with rubber band. Measure around lid; add 18". Cut a length of ribbon the determined measurement. Tie ribbon into a bow around lid, covering rubber band. Glue pick under knot of bow.
3. Line basket with excelsior. Place gift in basket.

A TASTE OF THE ORIENT

*B*ring a taste of the Far East to a friend's table this Christmas with our Oriental Broccoli Slaw Kit! Packed with flavor, the tangy, crunchy noodle mix will be a dinner delight. Tuck the medley into fancy fabric bags; then deliver your gift in a gilded basket along with serving instructions — and don't forget to include chopsticks and fortune cookies for all!

ORIENTAL BROCCOLI SLAW KIT

Broccoli slaw mix can be found with packaged salad greens.

- 1/4 cup butter
- 1 cup chopped walnuts
- 1 package (3 ounces) chicken-flavored ramen noodle soup mix
- 2 tablespoons vegetable oil
- 2 tablespoons sugar
- 2 tablespoons balsamic vinegar
- 2 tablespoons soy sauce
- 1/2 teaspoon ground black pepper
- 1 package (16 ounces) shredded broccoli slaw mix
- 1/2 cup sliced green onions

In a medium skillet over medium heat, melt butter. Add walnuts. Crush noodles and add to mixture. Stirring constantly, cook until mixture browns (about 10 minutes). Drain on paper towels; cool and set aside.

In a small saucepan, combine seasoning packet from ramen noodles, oil, sugar, vinegar, soy sauce, and pepper. Stirring constantly, cook over medium heat until sugar dissolves; cool.

In a large bowl, combine slaw mix and green onions. Place dressing mixture in an airtight container and noodle mixture and slaw mixture in separate resealable plastic bags; store in refrigerator. Give with serving instructions.

Yield: about 6 cups slaw mixture, about 2 cups noodle mixture, and about 1/2 cup dressing

To serve: Combine noodle mixture and slaw mixture in a large bowl. Add dressing; stir until well coated. Serve immediately.

Yield: about 7 cups slaw

ORIENTAL BASKET

You will need gold and red spray paint, basket (we used an 11" x 15" basket with handles), fabric for bags, 1/8" dia. wired gold cord, three artificial holly picks with berries, and fabric for liner.

1. Spray paint basket red; allow to dry. Lightly apply gold paint to basket; allow to dry.
2. Cut an 11" square from fabric for small bag, 9" x 30" piece from fabric for medium bag, and 13" x 37" piece from fabric for large bag and follow *Making a Fabric Bag*, page 154, to make each bag.
3. Fold top of each bag 2" to inside. Place gifts in bags. Tie a length of cord into a bow around top of each bag. Insert one pick under each bow.
4. Use fabric for liner and follow *Making a Basket Liner*, page 152, to make a liner with unfinished edges. Place liner and bags in basket.

LICKETY-SPLIT BEAN SOUP

A snappy complement for the holidays, our Easy Four-Bean Soup is a savory blend that's guaranteed to warm you up! A steaming hot bowl will melt away any winter blues and soothe the senses. To serve as a hearty meal for a special friend, package the soup in a sponge-painted gift bag.

EASY FOUR-BEAN SOUP

4	slices bacon
1½	cups chopped onions
1	can (4½ ounces) chopped green chiles
1	clove garlic, minced
2	cans (14½ ounces each) beef broth
1	can (16 ounces) pinto beans
1	can (16 ounces) navy beans
1	can (15.8 ounces) great Northern beans
1	can (15 ounces) black beans
1	can (10 ounces) diced tomatoes and green chiles
1	teaspoon ground cumin
1	teaspoon ground black pepper
½	teaspoon salt

In a Dutch oven, cook bacon over medium-low heat until crisp. Reserving drippings in skillet, drain bacon on paper towels and crumble. Increase heat to medium. Sauté onions, green chiles, and garlic in bacon drippings until onions are tender and begin to brown. Add beef broth, undrained beans, tomatoes and green chiles, cumin, pepper, salt, and bacon. Increase heat to medium high; bring mixture to a boil. Reduce heat to low; cover and simmer 30 minutes to let flavors blend. Serve warm.

Yield: about 12 cups soup

HOLLY BAG

You will need I, Q, V, X, Y, and period 1"h alphabet sponges; pink, red, green, and dark green acrylic paint; 7" x 9" brown gift bag; and holly motif tissue paper.

Allow paint to dry after each application.

1. Referring to Diagram for placement and using alphabet sponges, follow *Sponge Painting,* page 153, to paint red Q's; pink periods; dark green V's, X's, and Y's; and green I's on bag.

2. Line bag with tissue paper. Place gift in bag.

Diagram

MAGIC FUDGE

*C*oncocted in just a few minutes with ingredients you probably have on hand, our Magic Fudge Mix is a great last-minute gift for friends and neighbors. They'll love how easy it is to prepare: simply add water and pop the yummy mix into the microwave! Clothespins make adorable reindeer decorations when glued onto a gift bag. What a pleasing gift!

MAGIC FUDGE MIX

3¹/₂ cups confectioners sugar
¹/₂ cup cocoa
3 tablespoons non-dairy powdered creamer
¹/₄ teaspoon salt
¹/₂ cup butter or margarine, cut into pieces

In a large bowl, combine confectioners sugar, cocoa, creamer, and salt. Using a pastry blender or 2 knives, cut in butter until mixture is well blended. Store in an airtight container in refrigerator. Give with serving instructions.

Yield: about 4¹/₂ cups fudge mix

To serve: (*Note:* Recipe was tested in a 750-watt microwave.) Line an 8-inch square baking pan with aluminum foil, extending foil over 2 sides; grease foil. Combine fudge mix and ¹/₄ cup water in a large microwave-safe bowl. Microwave on high power (100%), stirring every 30 seconds, until mixture is smooth (about 3 minutes). Pour into prepared pan. Chill 1 hour or until firm. Use ends of foil to lift fudge from pan. Cut into 1-inch pieces. Store in an airtight container.

Yield: about 4 dozen pieces fudge

REINDEER BAG

You will need red acrylic paint, paintbrush, three flat wooden clothespins, hot glue gun, six 5mm wiggle eyes, three ¹/₄" dia. black pom-poms for noses, ¹/₂"w ribbon, 6" x 11" gift bag, 3¹/₂" x 5" piece of kraft paper, hole punch, and a black permanent fine-point marker.

1. For reindeer, paint clothespins red; allow to dry. Glue two eyes and one nose to each reindeer. Cut three 8" lengths of ribbon. Tie one length of ribbon into a bow around "antlers" of each reindeer. Arrange and glue reindeer on front of bag.

2. For tag, match short edges and fold kraft paper in half. Glue a 3¹/₂" length of ribbon along front bottom edge of tag. Punch hole in corner of tag. Use marker to write message on front of tag and serving instructions inside tag.

3. Place gift in bag. Fold top of bag 1³/₄" to back. Punch two holes 2" apart through center folded portion of bag. Thread a 20" length of ribbon through holes in bag and tag; tie into a bow at front of bag.

COOKS' CHOICE CHILI

*G*ive the gift of warmth this winter! Wrapped in beribboned plaid bags, this Chili Seasoning Mix is perfect for friends on the go. By adding ground beef and a few canned items to this mix, even a "non-cook" can create a hearty meal.

CHILI SEASONING MIX

- 1/2 cup chili powder
- 1/4 cup dried minced onions
- 2 tablespoons dried minced garlic
- 2 tablespoons ground cumin
- 2 tablespoons cornstarch
- 2 tablespoons salt
- 1 tablespoon sweet pepper flakes
- 1 tablespoon ground coriander
- 1 tablespoon ground black pepper
- 1 tablespoon dried cilantro
- 1 teaspoon dried oregano leaves
- 1/2 teaspoon ground red pepper
- 1/8 teaspoon ground cloves

In a small bowl, combine all ingredients; stir until well blended. Store in an airtight container. Give 1/4 cup seasoning mix with Chili recipe.

Yield: about 1 1/4 cups seasoning mix

CHILI

- 2 pounds ground beef
- 2 cans (8 ounces each) tomato sauce
- 1 can (16 ounces) pinto beans, undrained
- 1 can (14 1/2 ounces) diced tomatoes, undrained
- 1/4 cup Chili Seasoning Mix

In a large skillet, cook beef over medium heat until brown; drain meat. Stir

in tomato sauce, beans, tomatoes, and chili seasoning mix. Reduce heat to low. Stirring occasionally, cover and simmer 30 minutes. Serve warm.

Yield: about 7 cups chili

CHILI BAGS

For each bag, you will need a brown paper bag (we used 4" x 8" bags), paper-backed fusible web, fabric, photocopy of tag design (page 150) on ecru card stock, colored pencils, black permanent fine-point marker, spray adhesive, hole punch, and a 16" length of 5/8"w wired ribbon.

1. Draw around front of bag on paper side of web. Fuse web to wrong side of fabric; cut out along drawn line. Follow manufacturer's instructions to fuse fabric piece to front of bag.

2. With tag design at center, draw a 3" x 5" rectangle around tag; cut out along drawn lines. Use colored pencils to color tag. Use marker to write name on tag. Apply spray adhesive to wrong side of tag; smooth onto front of bag.

3. Place gift in bag. Fold top of bag 1 1/2" to back. Punch two holes 1" apart through center folded portion of bag. Thread ribbon through holes in folded portion of bag; tie into a bow at front of bag.

LOVIN' OVEN LOAF

Nothing says loving like something from the oven — especially when it's a fresh-baked loaf of bread! Our Orange Breakfast Loaf is a sweet way to jump-start anyone's day. Tuck the delicious treat in a basket and line with a cross-stitched towel. For a special touch, snuggle in a bag of their favorite coffee beans.

ORANGE BREAKFAST LOAF

$1/3$ cup butter or margarine, softened
$1^1/4$ cups sugar
1 container (8 ounces) sour cream
2 eggs
1 teaspoon orange extract
1 teaspoon grated orange zest
$1^3/4$ cups all-purpose flour
$1/2$ cup quick-cooking oats
1 teaspoon baking powder
$1/2$ teaspoon baking soda
$1/4$ teaspoon salt

Preheat oven to 350 degrees. Grease a $5^1/2$ x $9^1/2$-inch loaf pan. Line bottom of pan with waxed paper; grease waxed paper. In a large bowl, cream butter and sugar until fluffy. Add sour cream, eggs, orange extract, and orange zest; beat until smooth. In a small bowl, combine flour, oats, baking powder, baking soda, and salt. Add dry ingredients to creamed mixture; stir until well blended. Spread batter into prepared pan. Bake 55 to 60 minutes or until toothpick inserted in center of loaf comes out clean. Cool in pan 5 minutes. Remove from pan and cool completely on a wire rack. Store in an airtight container.

Yield: 1 loaf bread

"BELIEVE" CROSS-STITCHED TOWEL

You will need embroidery floss (see color key, page 131), kitchen towel with Aida insert (14 ct), and a basket (we used a 5" x 8" x 9" basket).

Refer to Cross Stitch, page 151, before beginning project.

1. Using three strands of floss for *Cross Stitches* and one strand of floss for *Backstitches* and *French Knots*, center and stitch design, page 131, on insert of towel.
2. Line basket with towel. Place gift in basket.

FROSTY CORN

A white Christmas always brings holiday cheer — and so will our White Chocolate Popcorn! Perfect for popcorn lovers, the sweet 'n' salty treat is definitely worth devouring. Deliver the crunchy snack in a lavishly detailed Victorian gift bag topped off with a dainty ribbon and frosted flowers.

WHITE CHOCOLATE POPCORN

24	cups popped popcorn
3/4	cup butter or margarine
2	cups firmly packed brown sugar
1/2	cup light corn syrup
1	teaspoon salt
1	teaspoon vanilla extract
1/2	teaspoon baking soda
8	ounces white candy coating, chopped
4	ounces white baking chocolate, chopped

Preheat oven to 250 degrees. Place popcorn in a lightly greased large roasting pan. In a heavy large saucepan, melt butter over medium heat. Stir in brown sugar, corn syrup, and salt. Stirring constantly, bring mixture to a boil. Boil 5 minutes without stirring. Remove from heat. Stir in vanilla and baking soda (mixture will foam). Pour syrup over popcorn; stir until well coated. Bake 1 hour, stirring every 15 minutes. Spread on lightly greased aluminum foil. In a small saucepan, melt candy coating and chocolate over low heat. Drizzle melted chocolate over popcorn. Let chocolate harden (about 30 minutes). Store popcorn in an airtight container.

Yield: about 27 cups popcorn

VICTORIAN BAG

You will need a brown paper bag (we used an 8 1/4" x 16" bag), Victorian-motif wrapping paper, spray adhesive, 2 3/4"w paper lace, craft knife, cutting mat, 1 1/3 yd. of 2 1/2"w sheer wired ribbon, 8" of craft wire, hot glue gun, and a frosted floral pick.

1. Measure height and width of bag; subtract 1/2" from each measurement. Cut a piece from wrapping paper the determined measurements. Apply spray adhesive to wrong side of paper; center and smooth onto front of bag.

2. Add 2" to width measurement of bag. Cut a length from lace the determined measurement. Fold top of bag 2 3/4" to front. Apply spray adhesive to wrong side of lace; center and smooth onto folded portion of bag.

3. Use craft knife to cut two 1" vertical slits 2" apart through center folded portion of bag. Place gift in bag; refold bag. Thread a 6" length of ribbon through slits; knot at front of bag. Use remaining ribbon and follow *Making a Bow*, page 153, to make a bow with two 6 1/2" loops, two 6" loops, a center loop, and two 8" streamers. Use wire to attach bow to knot of first ribbon. Hot glue pick under knot of bow.

COFFEE CONFECTIONS

Coffee lovers will think they've died and gone to heaven when they taste our tempting white chocolate-coated Coffee Patties! Drizzled with semisweet chocolate, the rich, creamy confections are not only delicious, they're also pretty! Wrap the candies in cellophane and tie with a festive plaid bow; then place the bag in a gold wire basket for a classy touch.

COFFEE PATTIES

- 2 tablespoons instant coffee granules
- 3 tablespoons coffee-flavored liqueur
- 1/2 cup butter or margarine, softened
- 1 teaspoon vanilla extract
- 1/4 teaspoon salt
- 4 cups confectioners sugar, divided
- 16 ounces white candy coating, chopped
- 6 ounces white baking chocolate, chopped
- 2/3 cup semisweet chocolate chips

In a small bowl, dissolve coffee granules in liqueur. In a large bowl, beat butter, vanilla, and salt until fluffy. Add coffee mixture to creamed mixture; beat until blended. Add 3³/4 cups confectioners sugar, beating until smooth. Shape mixture into 1-inch balls. Roll balls in remaining 1/4 cup confectioners sugar. Place balls on a baking sheet lined with waxed paper. Flatten balls to about 1/4-inch thickness with bottom of a glass dipped in confectioners sugar. Freeze 30 minutes or until firm.

Melt candy coating and chocolate in a heavy medium saucepan over low heat. Removing 6 patties at a time from freezer, dip patties into chocolate; return to a

second waxed paper-lined baking sheet. Let stand about 10 minutes or until coating hardens. Place chocolate chips in a small heavy-duty resealable plastic bag. Microwave on medium-high power (80%) 2¹/2 minutes or until chocolate melts, squeezing bag after each minute. Snip off 1 corner of bag to create a small opening. Drizzle over patties. Let chocolate harden. Store in an airtight container in refrigerator.

Yield: about 4 dozen patties

ORNAMENT BOW

You will need a 24" square of clear cellophane, rubber band, 18" of 1"w wired ribbon, hot glue gun, 1" dia. gold glass ball ornament, and a basket (we used a 4¹/4" x 7" decorative gold wire basket).

1. Place gift at center of cellophane. Gather cellophane over gift; secure gathers with rubber band.
2. Tie ribbon into a bow around gathers, covering rubber band. Glue top of ornament to knot of bow.
3. Place gift in basket.

TROPICAL INDULGENCE

An island getaway is just a few steps away…cooking steps, that is! A breeze to make, our Tropical Snowdrops are so dreamy and irresistible, your friends will think they're in paradise. Deliver the sweet confections — made with macadamias, fruits, and luscious white chocolate — in a jolly Santa jar. Then let the indulgence begin!

TROPICAL SNOWDROPS

- 8 ounces white candy coating, chopped
- 6 ounces white baking chocolate, chopped
- 1 jar (6½ ounces) macadamia nuts, coarsely chopped
- 1 cup flaked coconut
- 1 package (4 ounces) candied pineapple, chopped
- 1 package (4 ounces) red candied cherries, chopped

In a heavy large saucepan, melt candy coating and white chocolate over low heat. Remove from heat. Stir in nuts, coconut, and fruit. Drop by heaping teaspoonfuls onto a waxed paper-lined baking sheet. Chill about 30 minutes or until firm. Store in an airtight container in a cool place.

Yield: about 3½ dozen candies

SANTA JAR

You will need tracing paper; white, red, and black felt; hot glue gun; quart jar with lid; adult-size sock; 1¼" dia. gold jingle bell; basket (we used a 6" square wire and wooden basket); and white shredded paper.

1. Trace patterns, page 135, onto tracing paper; cut out. Using patterns, cut out beard, mustache, and two eyebrows from white felt; nose and mouth from red felt; and two eyes from black felt.
2. Arrange and glue face on jar.
3. Measuring from finished edge of cuff, cut a 6½" length from sock; discard toe. Gather cut edge of cuff; glue to secure. Glue bell to gathered end of hat. Place gift in jar. Place lid, then hat on jar.
4. Line basket with paper. Place gift in basket.

"BISQUE" WISHES

*M*ake a chilly winter night a bit warmer with our rich and creamy Broccoli-Cheese Bisque. Packed with flavor, this hearty soup contains healthy veggies and cheese — guaranteed to lift holiday spirits! Deliver a jar of the savory soup in a gift bag embellished with woodland appliqués, a festive bow, and a merry tag.

BROCCOLI-CHEESE BISQUE

- 1/2 cup chopped onion
- 2 cloves garlic, minced
- 2 tablespoons butter or margarine
- 3 cups milk, divided
- 1 can (14 1/2 ounces) chicken broth with roasted garlic
- 1 package (16 ounces) frozen chopped broccoli
- 1 cup coarsely chopped potato
- 1/2 cup sliced carrot
- 2 tablespoons all-purpose flour
- 1/2 teaspoon salt
- 1/2 teaspoon ground white pepper
- 1 container (16 ounces) pasteurized process cheese, cubed

Stirring constantly over medium heat, sauté onion and garlic in butter in a Dutch oven until lightly browned. Add 2 cups milk, chicken broth, broccoli, potato, and carrot. Increase heat to medium high and bring to a boil. Reduce heat to low; cover and simmer about 15 minutes or until vegetables are tender. Process mixture in batches in a food processor until smooth; return to Dutch oven over medium heat. In a small bowl, combine flour, salt, and white pepper. Gradually whisk remaining cup of milk into flour mixture; whisk until smooth. Whisking constantly, add milk mixture to soup; bring to a simmer. Continuing to whisk, simmer 3 minutes longer or until soup thickens slightly. Add cheese; whisk constantly until cheese melts. Serve warm or store in an airtight container in refrigerator.

Yield: about 8 1/4 cups soup

MOOSE BAG

You will need paper-backed fusible web, assorted fabrics, 8" x 10 1/2" gift bag with handles, hot glue gun, two 1/2" dia. buttons, two artificial holly leaves, decorative-edge craft scissors, corrugated craft cardboard, card stock, craft glue stick, black permanent fine-point marker, and tissue paper.

1. Use patterns, pages 132 and 133, and follow *Making Appliqués,* page 152, to make one each of star, tree, and moose appliqués from fabrics. Arrange and fuse appliqués on bag. Hot glue one button to star, leaves to neck of moose, and remaining button to leaves.
2. Tear a 1 1/2" x 14" strip from fabric. Tie strip into a bow around one handle of bag.
3. For tag, use craft scissors to cut one 2 1/2" x 3" piece from cardboard and one 1 7/8" x 2 3/8" piece from card stock. Use glue stick to glue card stock on cardboard. Use marker to draw border along edges and write message on tag. Use glue stick to glue tag to bag.
4. Line bag with tissue paper. Place gift in bag.

Chocolate lovers and coffee fans alike will beam about this java sensation! Cinnamon sticks dipped in a rich chocolate coating add holiday zest to a plain cup of "joe." For a wintry touch, wrap the stirrers in a cellophane bag, tie with a perky ribbon, and nestle in a frosted twig basket.

CHOCOLATE CINNAMON STIRRERS

$2/3$ cup semisweet chocolate chips
$1/8$ teaspoon cinnamon-flavored oil
   (used in candy making)
24 4-inch-long cinnamon sticks

In a small saucepan, melt chocolate chips over low heat. Remove from heat. Stir in flavored oil. Dip about $2/3$ of each cinnamon stick into melted chocolate. Place on a waxed paper-lined baking sheet. Chill about 30 minutes or until chocolate hardens.

Use cinnamon sticks to stir hot coffee or hot chocolate. Store in an airtight container in refrigerator.

Yield: 24 stirrers

SNOWY BASKET

You will need a stencil brush, textured snow medium, twig basket (we used a $3^1/2$" dia. basket), $4^3/4$" x 8" clear cellophane bag, 18" of 1"w satin ribbon, hot glue gun, and an artificial holly sprig.

1. Use stencil brush to apply snow medium along rim of basket; allow to dry.
2. Place gift in bag. Tie ribbon into a bow around top of bag. Glue holly to knot of bow.
3. Place bag in basket.

JUST PEACHY

Crunchy and crispy, our delicious Peach-Amaretto Biscotti is just "peachy!" These toast-like cookies are simply scrumptious when dipped in dessert wine, coffee, or cocoa. Festively display the homemade goodies in a basket detailed with colorful felt "penny rug" medallions.

PEACH-AMARETTO BISCOTTI

    1 package (7 ounces) dried peaches,
         finely chopped
  1/2 cup water
  1/2 cup amaretto
  1/2 cup butter or margarine, softened
    1 cup sugar
    2 eggs
    1 teaspoon almond extract
 31/2 cups all-purpose flour
    1 teaspoon baking powder
  1/2 teaspoon baking soda
  1/2 teaspoon ground nutmeg
  1/2 teaspoon salt

Combine peaches and water in a medium microwave-safe bowl. Cover and microwave on high power (100%) 2 minutes or until water boils. Stir in amaretto; cover and set aside.

Preheat oven to 350 degrees. In a large bowl, cream butter and sugar until fluffy. Add eggs and almond extract; beat until smooth. Stir in peach mixture. In a medium bowl, combine flour, baking powder, baking soda, nutmeg, and salt. Add dry ingredients to creamed mixture; stir until a soft dough forms. Divide dough in half. Grease and flour a baking sheet. Allowing 3 inches between loaves and flouring hands as necessary, shape each piece of dough into a 3 x 10-inch loaf.

Bake 35 to 40 minutes or until loaves are golden brown; cool 10 minutes on baking sheet. Cut loaves diagonally into 1/2-inch slices. Place slices flat on an ungreased baking sheet. Bake about 10 minutes or until surface is lightly browned. Turn slices over and bake 8 to 10 minutes longer or until surface is lightly browned. Transfer cookies to a wire rack to cool. Store in a cookie tin.

Yield: about 3 dozen cookies

"PENNY RUG" BASKET

You will need fabric for liner, basket (we used a 61/2" dia. basket with handle), 3/8"w and 5/8"w grosgrain ribbon, hot glue gun, tracing paper, pinking shears, assorted colors of felt, coordinating colors of embroidery floss, and one 1/2" dia. button for each star appliqué.

1. Use fabric and follow *Making a Basket Liner*, page 152, to make a liner with finished edges.

2. Measure around basket; add 1/2". Cut a length of each ribbon the determined measurement. Overlapping ends, center and glue 5/8"w ribbon, then 3/8"w ribbon around basket, at center of 5/8"w ribbon.

3. Trace patterns, page 134, onto tracing paper; cut out. For each medallion, use circle patterns and pinking shears to cut one large circle and one small circle from felt. Use star or tree pattern to cut design from felt.

4. Center small circle on large circle. Use one strand of floss to work *Running Stitches*, page 152, along edges of small circle to secure. Center design on small circle. Use one strand of floss to work *Running Stitches* along edges to secure. For star design, glue one button at center of star.

5. Glue medallions to ribbons on basket.

6. Place liner and gift in basket.

LET IT SNOW!

*L*et it snow, let it snow, let it snow! These Snowy Strawberry Squares are
a frosty reminder of summertime flavors. Paint a friendly snowman face on a
papier-mâché box to create a fitting carrier for a plateful of the frozen treats.

SNOWY STRAWBERRY SQUARES

- 1 cup all-purpose flour
- 1/4 cup firmly packed brown sugar
- 1/2 cup butter or margarine, softened
- 1/2 cup chopped pecans
- 1 package (10 ounces) frozen
     sweetened strawberries, thawed
- 1 cup granulated sugar
- 2 egg whites
- 2 tablespoons freshly squeezed lemon
     juice
- 1/8 teaspoon cream of tartar
- 1/2 cup whipping cream, whipped

Preheat oven to 350 degrees. In a small
bowl, combine flour, brown sugar, and
butter; stir until well blended. Stir in pecans.
Spread mixture into a 10 1/2 x 15 1/2-inch
jellyroll pan. Stirring occasionally, bake
about 12 minutes or until golden brown
and crumbly. Reserve 1/3 cup nut mixture;
sprinkle remainder into a greased
9 x 13-inch baking dish. Drain
strawberries, reserving 1/2 cup syrup.
In a double boiler over simmering water,
combine reserved strawberry syrup,
granulated sugar, egg whites, lemon juice,
and cream of tartar. Beat egg white
mixture at low speed of an electric mixer
until mixture reaches 160 degrees on a
thermometer (about 8 minutes). Pour
mixture into a large bowl; beat until soft
peaks form. Beat in strawberries. Fold in
whipped cream. Spoon filling over crust,
smoothing top. Sprinkle reserved nut
mixture over filling. Cover and freeze
overnight or until firm.

Cut into 2 1/2-inch squares. Transfer to
a serving plate. Cover and store in freezer.

Yield: about 15 servings

PAINTED SNOWMAN BOX

You will need white, orange, pink, grey,
and dark grey acrylic paint; paintbrushes;
natural sea sponge; 2" x 5" wooden heart;
hot glue gun; 1" dia. piece of household
sponge; 7 1/2" x 20" piece of fabric; paper
towels; and a toothbrush.

*Refer to Painting Techniques, page 153,
before beginning project. Allow paint to
dry after each application.*

1. Paint box and lid white. Use natural
sponge to lightly sponge paint box and lid
grey. For nose, use paintbrush to paint
heart orange.
2. Using lid for snowman's face, use
natural sponge to lightly paint pink
cheeks, household sponge to paint grey
eyebrows and dark grey eyes and mouth,
and end of paintbrush to add a white
highlight to each eye. Glue nose to face.
3. For scarf, fringe one end of fabric 3/4".
Tie a knot in scarf 6" from fringed end;
arrange and glue scarf on box.
4. Spatter paint snowman and
scarf white.

HOLIDAY "SPIRITS"

*O*ur fruity "spirits" will lift the hearts of your friends and family! A glass of Orange-Tangerine Wine is a perfect pick-me-up during the hectic holiday season. Using a blend of white wine, juice concentrate, and flavored liqueur, this citrusy cordial can be concocted in no time at all! Give your gift with style in an elegant tasseled bottle bag.

ORANGE-TANGERINE WINE

  1 cup water
  ½ cup sugar
  1 bottle (1.5 liters) dry white wine
  ½ cup frozen orange-tangerine juice
        concentrate, thawed
  ½ cup orange-flavored liqueur

Combine water and sugar in a small saucepan. Stirring constantly, cook over medium heat until sugar dissolves. In a 1-gallon container, combine wine, juice concentrate, liqueur, and sugar mixture. Stir until well blended. Pour into gift bottles with corks. Store in refrigerator. Serve chilled.

Yield: about 9 cups wine

TASSELED BOTTLE BAG

You will need an 18" x 20" fabric place mat, rubber band, 36" of beaded rope with a tassel at each end, hot glue gun, assorted beads, and a 4" long stick pin.

1. Matching right sides and long edges, follow *Making a Fabric Bag*, page 154, to make a bag from place mat.
2. Place bottle (from recipe this page) in bag. Gather bag around neck of bottle; secure with rubber band. Wrap rope

around bottle twice, covering rubber band. Overlap rope ends on front of bag. Glue to secure.

3. Thread beads onto pin. Insert pin into cork stopper.

LEMON DELIGHTS

Spread season's greetings with our light and crispy Lemon Lace Cookies! These delectable confections have a delicate lemon flavor that's just right. Present the sweet sensations in a gold basket accented with white tulle and a pretty poinsettia.

LEMON LACE COOKIES

2	cups butter or margarine, softened
1¼	cups sugar
1	tablespoon grated lemon zest
1	teaspoon lemon extract
1	teaspoon vanilla extract
3	cups quick-cooking oats
2	cups all-purpose flour
½	teaspoon salt
	Confectioners sugar

In a large bowl, cream butter and sugar until fluffy. Beat in lemon zest and extracts. In a medium bowl, combine oats, flour, and salt. Add dry ingredients to creamed mixture; stir until a soft dough forms. Cover and chill 30 minutes.

Preheat oven to 350 degrees. Shape dough into 1-inch balls; place about 2 inches apart on an ungreased baking sheet. Flatten balls with bottom of glass dipped in confectioners sugar. Bake 9 to 11 minutes or until edges are lightly browned. Cool cookies on baking sheet 1 minute; transfer to a wire rack to cool completely. Store in an airtight container.

Yield: about 8 dozen cookies

WHITE POINSETTIA BASKET

You will need two 6" x 30" strips of white tulle, 7" dia. gold basket, hot glue gun, and a large artificial white-flocked poinsettia.

1. Arrange strips of tulle on a flat surface to form a cross (Fig. 1).

Fig. 1

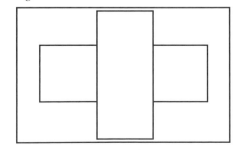

2. Place basket at center of crossed strips of tulle.
3. Place gift in basket.
4. Knot ends of tulle over basket.
5. Glue poinsettia to knot of tulle.

FRUITCAKE FANCIES

Our Fruitcake Caramels take the cake — and you don't even need a fork to eat them! These chewy bites are filled with all the flavorful fixings of the traditional wintertime favorite. Package the sweets in button-trimmed tree bags for a pleasing presentation.

FRUITCAKE CARAMELS

- 2 cups sugar
- 1$^{1}/_{2}$ cups whipping cream, divided
- 1 cup light corn syrup
- $^{1}/_{4}$ cup butter
- $^{1}/_{3}$ cup chopped red candied cherries
- $^{1}/_{3}$ cup chopped green candied cherries
- $^{1}/_{3}$ cup chopped candied pineapple
- $^{1}/_{2}$ cup chopped pecans, toasted
- 1 teaspoon vanilla extract

Line a 9 x 13-inch baking pan with aluminum foil, extending foil over ends of pan; grease foil. Butter sides of a heavy Dutch oven. Combine sugar, $^{3}/_{4}$ cup whipping cream, corn syrup, and butter in Dutch oven. Stirring constantly, cook over medium-low heat until sugar dissolves. Using a pastry brush dipped in hot water, wash down any sugar crystals on sides of pan. Attach a candy thermometer to pan, making sure thermometer does not touch bottom of pan. Increase heat to medium; continue to stir and bring syrup to a boil. Gradually stir in remaining $^{3}/_{4}$ cup whipping cream. Stirring frequently, cook until mixture reaches firm-ball stage (approximately 242 to 248 degrees). Test about $^{1}/_{2}$ teaspoon mixture in ice water. Mixture will roll into a firm ball in ice water but

will flatten if pressed when removed from water. Remove from heat; stir in fruit, pecans, and vanilla. Pour mixture into prepared pan. Cool several hours at room temperature.

Use ends of foil to lift candy from pan. Use a lightly oiled heavy knife to cut candies into 1-inch squares. Wrap candies individually in waxed paper and store in an airtight container in a cool place.

Yield: about 8 dozen caramels

CUTOUT TREE BAGS

For each bag, you will need paper-backed fusible web, green fabric, poster board, hot glue gun, brown lunch-size paper bag, assorted buttons, hole punch, and raffia.

1. Use pattern, page 132, and follow *Making Appliqués*, page 152, to make two tree appliqués (one in reverse) from green fabric. Fuse trees to poster board; cut out.
2. Aligning bottoms of trees with bottom of bag, glue one tree to each side of bag.
3. Cutting to within 3$^{1}/_{2}$" from bottom of bag, cut front and back of bag along tree edges and across sides of bag.
4. Arrange and glue buttons to front of tree bag as desired. Punch two holes $^{1}/_{2}$" apart at center top of trees.
5. Place gift in bag. Thread a 20" length of raffia through holes in bag; tie into a bow at front of bag.

MERRY MEALS

*B*oggle *their eyes and delight their taste buds with these creative hamburger look-alikes! Filled with tinted coconut and chocolate frosting, our Sugar Cookie "Burgers" are a merry treat that everyone will enjoy. Small snackers who are always on the go will especially like the scrumptious sweets in a "take-out" bag straight from the North Pole!*

SUGAR COOKIE "BURGERS"

Cookies are best when given the day they are made.

    1 package (18 ounces) refrigerated
          sugar cookie dough
  1/4 cup chopped peanuts
1 1/2 cups flaked coconut
          Green liquid food coloring
    1 container (16 ounces) chocolate
          ready-to-spread frosting

Preheat oven to 350 degrees. Cut cookie dough into 1/4-inch slices. Place 2 inches apart on an ungreased baking sheet; shape into rounds. On half of cookies, press 1/2 teaspoon peanuts into each cookie. Bake 8 to 10 minutes or until tops are lightly browned. Transfer cookies to a wire rack to cool.

Place coconut in a resealable plastic bag. Add 5 to 6 drops food coloring. Shake coconut until evenly tinted; set aside. Spread 1 tablespoon frosting over flat side of each plain cookie; sprinkle about 1 1/2 tablespoons coconut over frosting. Spread 1 teaspoon frosting over flat side of each peanut cookie. Place peanut cookies on coconut-covered cookies; gently squeeze cookies together. Store in an airtight container.
Yield: about 16 cookie "burgers"

MERRY MEAL BAGS

F*or each bag,* you will need a 6" x 11" gift bag, hole punch, two 24" lengths each of two colors of curling ribbon, photocopy of tag design (page 149) on white card stock, craft glue stick, and one 4 3/4" x 6" sheet of self-adhesive stickers.

1. Place gift in bag. Fold top of bag 2" to back. At each side of bag, punch a hole through center folded portion of bag. Thread one ribbon of each color through hole; tie together into a bow. Curl ribbon ends.
2. Cut out tag; glue at top center front of bag. Glue corners of sticker sheet to front of bag.

65

LUMBERJACK CHEESE BASKET

Our hearty Lumberjack Cheese Logs boast a bold flavor that's big enough for appetites the size of Paul Bunyan's! Flavored with sharp Cheddar, bacon, and pecans, the zippy spread is sure to satisfy serious snackers. Present each log in a rustic basket along with some crackers.

LUMBERJACK CHEESE LOGS

4 cups (16 ounces) shredded sharp Cheddar cheese

4 ounces cream cheese, softened

1 tablespoon prepared horseradish

6 slices bacon, cooked and crumbled

2 tablespoons plus 2 teaspoons chopped fresh dill weed, divided

1 cup finely chopped pecans, toasted
    Crackers to serve

Process cheeses and horseradish in a food processor until well blended. Add bacon and 2 tablespoons dill weed; pulse process until blended. Shape into two 6-inch-long rolls. In a small bowl, combine pecans and remaining 2 teaspoons dill weed. Press pecan mixture onto cheese rolls. Wrap in plastic wrap and store in refrigerator. Serve with crackers.

Yield: 2 cheese logs, about 1¼ cups each

TIMBERMAN'S BASKET

You will need flannel fabric for liner, basket (we used an 8" x 15" basket with handles), 11" x 12" piece of fabric for bag, paper-backed fusible web, fabric scraps for appliqués and tag, decorative-edge craft scissors, black permanent fine-point marker, three 16" lengths of natural raffia, hot glue gun, artificial pinecone, several artificial evergreen sprigs, pinking shears, craft glue, 2³/₄" x 4" piece of corrugated craft cardboard, 1³/₄" x 3" piece of brown card stock, hole punch, 6¼" x 13³/₄" wooden cutting board, and a 10" miniature hand saw.

1. Use fabric for liner and follow *Making a Basket Liner*, page 152, to make a liner with finished edges.

2. Use fabric for bag and follow *Making a Fabric Bag*, page 154, to make a bag.

3. Use patterns, page 141, and follow *Making Appliqués*, page 152, to make one each of tree, trunk, moon, and star appliqués from fabric scraps (use craft scissors to cut out tree appliqué). Arrange and fuse appliqués on bag. Use marker to draw "stitches" along edges of star and moon appliqués.

4. Place gift in bag. Knot two strands of raffia around top of bag. Hot glue pinecone to knot of raffia. Tuck several evergreen sprigs under raffia.

5. For tag, use pinking shears to cut a 2¼" x 3½" piece from fabric scrap. Use craft glue to glue fabric piece to cardboard, then card stock to fabric piece; allow to dry. Use marker to draw "stitches" along edges and write message on card stock. Punch hole in tag. Use remaining raffia to attach tag to basket.

6. Place liner, remaining evergreen sprigs, bag, cutting board, and saw in basket.

A TASTE "YULE" LOVE

*W*hip up a batch of our Orange Chip Cookies for a taste we know "yule" love! The heavenly blend of white chocolate and orange is sure to be a hit when shared among friends. Snuggle the merry morsels in a beribboned basket lined with a hand-stitched bread cover for a charming touch.

ORANGE CHIP COOKIES

    1   cup butter or margarine, softened
1 1/4   cups sugar
    1   egg
    1   tablespoon grated orange zest
    2   teaspoons orange extract
2 1/4   cups all-purpose flour
  3/4   teaspoon baking soda
  1/2   teaspoon salt
    1   package (12 ounces) white baking
        chips
    1   cup chopped walnuts, toasted

Preheat oven to 350 degrees. In a large bowl, cream butter and sugar until fluffy. Add egg, orange zest, and orange extract. Beat until well blended. In a medium bowl, combine flour, baking soda, and salt. Add dry ingredients to creamed mixture; stir until a soft dough forms. Stir in baking chips and walnuts. Drop tablespoonfuls of dough onto a greased baking sheet. Bake 8 to 10 minutes or until edges are lightly browned. Transfer cookies to a wire rack to cool. Store in an airtight container.

Yield: about 4 1/2 dozen cookies

COOKIE BASKET

You will need embroidery floss (see color key, page 142), white Royal Classic Bread Cover (14 ct), basket with handle (we used an 8 1/2" dia. basket), 20" of 1 1/2"w wired ribbon, hot glue gun, and an artificial holly sprig with berries.

Refer to Cross Stitch, page 151, before beginning project.

1. Using three strands of floss for *Cross Stitches* and one strand of floss for *Backstitches* and *French Knots*, stitch design, page 142, at one corner of bread cover 3/4" from outer edges of fringe.
2. Place bread cover in basket. Tie ribbon into a bow around handle. Glue holly sprig to knot of bow.

SPLENDID SPREAD

During the hectic holiday season, friends will enjoy a relaxing happy-hour at home with this quick-to-fix snack. Our Smoked Turkey Spread is a guaranteed taste bud pleaser! Share a bowl of the savory spread in a white basket adorned with pretty poinsettias. Be sure to include crackers for a crunchy complement!

SMOKED TURKEY SPREAD

- 1 package (8 ounces) cream cheese, softened
- 1 cup chopped smoked turkey
- 1/4 cup mayonnaise
- 2/3 cup chopped pecans, toasted and divided
- 6 tablespoons chopped fresh parsley, divided
- 1/8 teaspoon ground red pepper
    Crackers to serve

Process cream cheese, turkey, and mayonnaise in a food processor until well blended. Add 1/2 cup pecans, 4 tablespoons parsley, and red pepper. Pulse process until blended. Spoon into small bowl; garnish with remaining pecans and 2 tablespoons parsley. Cover and store in refrigerator. Serve with crackers.

Yield: about 2 1/4 cups spread

WHITE BASKET WITH POINSETTIAS

You will need wire cutters, 4" dia. artificial poinsettias, hot glue gun, white basket (we used an 8" x 10 1/2" basket with handle), and tissue paper.

1. Use wire cutters to cut poinsettias and leaves from stems. Glue flowers and leaves around rim of basket.

2. Line basket with tissue paper. Place gift in basket.

69

easy!

PECAN LOVERS' PICK

Pick these Lemon-Rosemary Pecans for nut lovers! The zesty toasted treats are sure to be a glorious snack. Pack the nuts in a pretty wax-sealed bag for delivery.

LEMON-ROSEMARY PECANS

  4 cups pecan halves
$^1/_3$ cup butter
  3 to 4 tablespoons finely chopped
       fresh rosemary
  1 tablespoon white wine
       Worcestershire sauce
  2 teaspoons grated lemon zest
  1 teaspoon lemon pepper
$^1/_2$ teaspoon salt

Preheat oven to 250 degrees. Place pecans in a medium bowl. In a small microwave-safe bowl, combine butter, rosemary, white wine Worcestershire sauce, lemon zest, lemon pepper, and salt; microwave until butter melts. Pour over pecans, tossing until well coated. Spread pecans on an ungreased jellyroll pan. Bake 45 minutes or until pecans are toasted. Cool in pan. Store in an airtight container.

Yield: about 4 cups pecans

WAX-SEALED BAGS

For each bag, you will need a 4" x 8" brown paper bag, spray adhesive, $3^1/_4$" x $16^1/_2$" piece of wrapping paper, 6" of $^1/_2$"w satin ribbon, hot glue gun, gold sealing wax, and an embossing seal.

1. Fold top of bag 2" to front; crease, then unfold. Apply spray adhesive to wrong side of wrapping paper. Beginning at top

back of bag, smooth paper on bag from back to front.
2. Place gift in bag. Cross ends of ribbon to form a loop at center of ribbon; glue to

secure. Glue loop to front of bag.
3. Following manufacturer's instructions, melt a puddle of sealing wax over crossed portion of ribbon. Apply seal to wax; remove seal. Allow wax to cool.

SPICY ICY COFFEE

*O*ur *Fiery Iced Coffee Mix is a flavorful way to send season's greetings to a treasured friend! The unique blend of sugar and spices has a surprising ingredient — red pepper. Although this coffee may taste spicy-hot, it's served chilled over ice. Give the refreshing drink mix in plaid ribbon bags.*

FIERY ICED COFFEE MIX

- 1 cup instant coffee granules
- 1 cup non-dairy powdered creamer
- 1/2 cup sugar
- 1 teaspoon ground cinnamon
- 1/2 teaspoon ground nutmeg
- 1/2 teaspoon ground red pepper
- 1/4 teaspoon ground cardamom

Process all ingredients in a food processor until well blended. Store in an airtight container. Give with serving instructions.

Yield: about 2 cups mix

To serve: Pour 8 ounces boiling water over 2 tablespoons mix; stir until well blended. Cool and serve chilled over ice.

RIBBON BAGS

For each bag, you will need 18" of 3⅝"w wired satin ribbon, 24" of ⅛" dia. green cord, 15" of ¹⁄₁₆" dia. red cord, hot glue gun, artificial holly sprig with berries, and a 1" dia. ball ornament.

1. Matching wrong sides and short edges, fold ribbon in half. Stitch sides of ribbon together.
2. Place gift in bag.

3. Tie cord lengths together into a bow around top of bag; knot ends of cord.

Glue holly sprig and ornament to knot of bow.

STARBURST BREAD

*O*ur Starburst Bread is bursting with cheer! The blissful bread makes a tasty complement to Christmas dinner, or it would be delicious served warm with butter for a late-night snack! For a charming presentation, display the star-shaped bread in a lined basket trimmed with festive ribbons.

STARBURST BREAD

    2 tablespoons sugar
    1 package dry yeast
1 1/4 cups warm water
  1/3 cup vegetable oil
    3 tablespoons honey
1 1/4 teaspoons salt
  1/8 teaspoon ground turmeric
    2 eggs
    5 to 5 1/2 cups all-purpose flour,
       divided
       Vegetable oil cooking spray

In a small bowl, dissolve sugar and yeast in 1 1/4 cups warm water. In a large bowl, combine oil, honey, salt, and turmeric. Add eggs and yeast mixture to oil mixture; beat until well blended. Add 4 cups flour; stir until a soft dough forms. Turn dough onto a lightly floured surface. Knead about 5 minutes or until dough becomes smooth and elastic, using additional flour as necessary. Place in a large bowl sprayed with cooking spray, turning once to coat top of dough. Cover and let rise in a warm place (80 to 85 degrees) 1 1/2 hours or until doubled in size.

Turn dough onto a lightly floured surface and punch down. Cover dough and allow to rest 10 minutes. Place dough in a greased 13-inch star-shaped cake pan, pressing dough into corners. Make slashes in dough from center to end of each point. Spray top of dough with cooking spray. Cover and let rise in a warm place 1 hour or until doubled in size.

Preheat oven to 375 degrees. Bake 18 to 25 minutes or until loaf is golden brown and sounds hollow when tapped. Cover with aluminum foil if bread browns too quickly. Serve warm or transfer to a wire rack to cool. Store in an airtight container.

Yield: 1 loaf bread

BREAD BASKET LINER AND BOW

You will need fabric, basket with handles (we used a 15" dia. basket), 36" of mesh wired ribbon, and 24" of 1/2"w metallic ribbon.

1. Use fabric and follow *Making a Basket Liner*, page 152, to make a liner with finished edges. Place liner in basket.
2. Use wired ribbon and follow *Making a Bow*, page 153, to make a bow with four 6" loops and two 6" streamers. Use metallic ribbon to attach bow to one handle of basket.
3. Place liner and gift in basket.

DELECTABLY ELEGANT

For a truly elegant way to convey Yuletide wishes, offer a warm pan of delectable Cranberry-Pear Rolls. The crowning touch for the gilded sleeve is a miniature grapevine wreath accented with garland, berries, and shimmering ribbon.

CRANBERRY-PEAR ROLLS

     2 cups sugar
     2 cups water
   1/2 cup butter or margarine, melted
  2 1/2 cups all-purpose flour
  2 3/4 teaspoons baking powder
   1/2 teaspoon salt
   3/4 cup vegetable shortening
   1/2 cup milk
     1 egg, beaten
  1 1/2 teaspoons vanilla extract
     3 cups finely chopped ripe pears
        (about 3 large pears)
     1 package (6 ounces) sweetened
        dried cranberries, chopped
  1 1/4 teaspoons apple pie spice

In a heavy medium saucepan, combine sugar and water over medium-high heat. Stirring frequently, bring to a boil and cook until sugar dissolves; set aside to cool.

Preheat oven to 350 degrees. Pour melted butter into two 8-inch square aluminum foil baking pans (with plastic lids). In a medium bowl, combine flour, baking powder, and salt. Using a pastry blender or 2 knives, cut shortening into dry ingredients until mixture resembles coarse meal. Add milk, egg, and vanilla; stir just until moistened. On a lightly floured surface, use a floured rolling pin to roll out dough to a 10 x 18-inch rectangle. Sprinkle pears and cranberries over dough to within 1 inch of edges. Sprinkle apple pie spice over fruit. Beginning at 1 long edge, carefully roll up dough jellyroll style. Pinch seam to seal. Cut roll into 1-inch slices. Place in pans with cut side down and sides touching. Pour syrup over dough. Bake uncovered 50 to 60 minutes or until golden brown. Serve warm.

Yield: 2 pans rolls, about 9 rolls in each pan

DECORATED PAPER SLEEVE

You will need spray adhesive, 6" x 26" piece each of poster board and wrapping paper, ruler, straight edge scissors, 8" square x 2"h aluminum pan with lid, clear tape, hot glue gun, artificial miniature leaf garland, artificial miniature berry pick, 4" dia. grapevine wreath, and 20" of 1/2"w wired ribbon.

1. For sleeve, apply spray adhesive to one side of poster board; smooth onto wrong side of wrapping paper.
2. Using ruler and one point of scissors, score wrong side of sleeve 6" and 8 1/2" from each short edge. Folding along scored lines and overlapping ends at bottom of pan, wrap sleeve around pan; tape to secure.
3. Hot glue garland and berries to wreath. Tie ribbon into a bow around top of wreath. Hot glue wreath to sleeve.

CHOCOLATE YUMMIES

*C*rispy, chocolaty, and oh-so-yummy, our Fruit and Toasted Nut Clusters are chock-full of flavor. *The delightful delicacies are a combination of cranberries and toasted pecans covered with luscious chocolate — a sweet tooth's dream! Present the morsels in a cheery stuffed snowman basket.*

FRUIT AND TOASTED NUT CLUSTERS

- 16 ounces white candy coating, chopped
- 1 package (11½ ounces) milk chocolate chips
- 3 cups chopped pecans, toasted
- 1 package (6 ounces) sweetened dried cranberries, chopped

In a heavy large saucepan, combine candy coating and chocolate chips. Stirring constantly, melt chocolate over low heat. Remove from heat; stir in pecans and cranberries. Drop by heaping teaspoonfuls onto baking sheets lined with waxed paper. Let stand at room temperature until firm. Store in a single layer in an airtight container in a cool place.

Yield: about 6 dozen candies

SNOWMAN BASKET

You will need tracing paper, muslin, transfer paper, polyester fiberfill, red and black acrylic paint, paintbrushes, basket (we used a 6" x 7¼" x 4" basket), ⅞"w wired ribbon, hot glue gun, two 1" dia. red pom-poms, 7" of black chenille stem, ¼" dia. red pom-pom, artificial holly sprig with berries, black dimensional paint, and tissue paper.

Match right sides and raw edges and use a ¼" seam allowance for all stitching.

1. Trace patterns, page 130, onto tracing paper; cut out. Using patterns, cut two head, four arm, and four leg pieces from muslin. Leaving an opening for turning, stitch two pieces of each shape together to make one head, two arms, and two legs. Clip curves and turn pieces right side out. Use transfer paper to transfer face to head.
2. Stuff head and arms with fiberfill; stitch openings closed. Stuff lower half of each leg with fiberfill. Knot each leg at center for "knee." Stuff remaining half of each leg; stitch opening closed.
3. Use acrylic paint to paint red "gloves" on arms and black "shoes" on legs; allow to dry.
4. Measure around basket; add 22". Cut a length of ribbon the determined measurement. Wrap ribbon around rim of basket and tie into a bow at front of basket; spot glue to secure. Position head at outside center back of basket; glue to secure. Position top of arms below head and glue arms around rim of basket. Glue tops of legs to bottom front of basket.
5. For earmuffs, glue one 1" dia. pom-pom to each end of chenille stem. Shape earmuffs over head; glue to secure. Glue ¼" pom-pom to face for nose and holly sprig to "neck." Use dimensional paint to paint eyes and mouth; allow to dry.
6. Line basket with tissue paper. Place gift in basket.

RITZY SPRITZ

*R*ich and buttery, our *Chocolate Spritz Cookies will bring smiles to the cookie lovers on your list! Not only are these bites delicious, they're also cute — the Scottie dog shapes are easy to create by using a cookie press. Deliver the scrumptious sweets in a decorated Scottie dog bag for a yummy Yuletide gift!*

CHOCOLATE SPRITZ COOKIES

- 1 cup butter or margarine, softened
- 1 package (3 ounces) cream cheese
- $2/3$ cup sugar
- 1 egg
- 2 teaspoons vanilla extract
- 3 ounces semisweet baking chocolate, melted and cooled
- 3 cups all-purpose flour
- $1/4$ teaspoon salt
- 1 tube ($4^{1}/_{4}$ ounces) red decorating icing

Preheat oven to 375 degrees. In a large bowl, cream butter, cream cheese, and sugar until fluffy. Add egg and vanilla; beat until smooth. Beat in melted chocolate. In a medium bowl, combine flour and salt. Add dry ingredients to creamed mixture; beat until well blended. Spoon dough into a cookie press fitted with a $1^{7}/_{8}$-inch Scottie dog template. Press cookies onto an ungreased baking sheet. Bake 5 to 7 minutes or until bottoms are very lightly browned. Transfer cookies to a wire rack to cool. Transfer icing into a pastry bag fitted with a small round tip. Pipe bow onto each cookie. Let icing harden. Store in an airtight container.

Yield: about 14 dozen cookies

SCOTTIE DOG BAG

You will need a brown lunch-size paper bag, decorative-edge craft scissors, plaid wrapping paper, hot glue gun, three $3/4$" dia. black buttons, tracing paper, black corrugated craft cardboard, card stock to coordinate with wrapping paper, and 6" of $1/2$"w satin ribbon.

1. For flap, fold top of bag $1^{1}/_2$" to front. Measure width of bag. Use craft scissors to cut a strip from wrapping paper 1" wide by the determined measurement. Glue strip along bottom edge of flap. Arrange and glue buttons on strip.

2. Trace dog pattern, page 147, onto tracing paper; cut out. Draw around pattern on cardboard; cut out.
3. Use craft scissors to cut one 4" x $4^{1}/_2$" piece from card stock and one $3^{1}/_2$" x 4" piece from wrapping paper. Center and glue dog on wrapping paper, then wrapping paper on card stock. Glue card stock on bag.
4. Tie ribbon into a bow. Glue bow on dog.
5. Place gift in bag; glue flap closed.

MERRY MOUNTAIN MIX

*E*ven your favorite outdoorsman needs a break from the rugged terrain to enjoy a refreshing treat! Satisfy the cravings of woodland scouts with our sweet and crunchy Mountain Trail Mix — an energy-rich blend of fruits, nuts, and oat cereal. Package the mix in a colorful gift bag.

MOUNTAIN TRAIL MIX

- 3 cups honey-nut round toasted oat cereal
- 1 cup sunflower kernels
- 1 cup sliced almonds
- 1 cup flaked coconut
- 1 cup sweetened dried cranberries
- 1 cup finely chopped dried apples
- 1 cup golden raisins
- 1 can (14 ounces) sweetened condensed milk

Preheat oven to 300 degrees. In a large bowl, combine cereal, sunflower kernels, almonds, coconut, cranberries, apples, and raisins. Pour sweetened condensed milk over mixture; stir until well coated. Transfer to a greased $10^1/_2$ x $15^1/_2$-inch jellyroll pan. Bake 45 to 50 minutes or until mixture begins to dry and is golden brown, stirring every 10 minutes. Transfer to aluminum foil to cool. Break into pieces. Store in an airtight container in refrigerator.

Yield: about 11 cups trail mix

SLED BAG

You will need a gift bag with handles (we used an 8" x 10" bag), Southwestern-motif wrapping paper, spray adhesive, several 1 yd. lengths of red raffia, hot glue gun, artificial pine sprigs with pinecones, black permanent fine-point marker, miniature wooden sled, craft wire, and wire cutters.

1. Measure height and width of bag; subtract $1/_2$" from each measurement. Cut a piece from wrapping paper the determined measurements. Apply spray adhesive to wrong side of wrapping paper; center and smooth onto front of bag.

2. Place gift in bag. Tie raffia into a bow around one handle of bag. Hot glue sprigs to knot of bow.

3. Use marker to write message on sled. Use craft wire to attach sled to sprigs.

"PICKLED" PINK

*Y*our friends will be "pickled" pink to receive our delicious Fiesta Pickles! A cinch to make, the pickles boast a sweet and zesty flavor with an unforgettable crunch. Give the tasty treats in a jar topped with a festive fabric lid. Deliver in a bag adorned with a homemade gift tag, and don't forget to button it with love!

FIESTA PICKLES

- 1 gallon hamburger dill pickle slices, drained
- 6 cups sugar
- 1/2 cup freshly squeezed lime juice
- 4 cloves garlic, minced
- 1 teaspoon hot pepper sauce
- 1 teaspoon ground cumin
- 1 teaspoon ground turmeric

In a very large nonmetal bowl, combine pickles, sugar, lime juice, garlic, pepper sauce, cumin, and turmeric. Stir until sugar begins to dissolve. Return pickles to gallon jar. Seal tightly with jar lid. Store pickles at room temperature 48 hours or until sugar dissolves, inverting jar twice a day. Store in refrigerator; serve chilled.

Yield: about 16 cups pickles

BAG AND JAR SETS

For each set, you will need a pint jar with lid, fabric, pinking shears, rubber band, raffia, brown lunch-size paper bag, stapler, 1" dia. wooden button, black embroidery floss, hot glue gun, colored pencils, photocopy of tag design (page 149) on ecru card stock, black

permanent fine-point marker, and a hole punch.

1. Draw around lid on wrong side of fabric. Use pinking shears to cut out circle 2" outside drawn line. Center circle over lid; secure with rubber band. Measure around lid; add 18". Cut several lengths of raffia the determined measurement. Tie raffia together into a bow around lid, covering rubber band.

2. Place jar in bag. Fold bag 1 1/2" to front; staple through center folded portion to secure. Knotting at back of button, thread a length of floss through holes in button; trim floss close to button. Glue button to bag, covering staple.

3. Use pencils to color tag and marker to write message on tag; cut out. Punch hole in corner of tag. Thread one 6" length of raffia through hole in tag; knot ends to form a loop. Use loop to hang tag from button.

CHEERY CHEESE DIP

This South-of-the-Border sensation will no doubt spice up the Yuletide season! Served warm with tortilla chips, our White Cheese Dip makes a splendid snack for all your favorite merry munchers. For a praiseworthy presentation, nestle a hand-labeled canister of dip, along with a bag of chips, in an excelsior-lined birch-bark basket.

WHITE CHEESE DIP

- 1/4 cup butter or margarine
- 1/4 cup all-purpose flour
- 1 tablespoon ground cumin
- 1 teaspoon garlic salt
- 1/4 teaspoon dry mustard
- 2 cups half and half
- 2 tablespoons chopped pickled jalapeño peppers
- 2 teaspoons juice from pickled jalapeño peppers
- 2 cups (8 ounces) shredded white American cheese
  Tortilla chips to serve

In a large saucepan, melt butter over medium heat. Stir in flour, cumin, garlic salt, and dry mustard. Stirring constantly, cook 1 minute. Gradually stir in half and half. Stirring constantly, cook about 5 minutes or until mixture thickens. Stir in peppers, pepper juice, and cheese. Cook until cheese melts and mixture is smooth. Serve warm with tortilla chips. Store in an airtight container in refrigerator.

Yield: about 3 cups dip

CHEESE DIP BASKET

You will need colored pencils, photocopy of label design (page 150) on ecru card stock, spray adhesive, airtight container to accommodate label, 6" x 11" gift bag, stapler, red raffia, hot glue gun, 1" dia. wooden button, basket (we used a 9" x 13" oval birch-bark basket with handles), and natural excelsior.

1. Use pencils to color label. Cut out label. Apply spray adhesive to wrong side of label; smooth onto side of container.

2. Place chips in bag. Fold top of bag 2" to front; staple through center folded portion to secure. Cut several 28" lengths of raffia. Tie raffia together into a bow. Hot glue bow to front of bag, covering staple. Hot glue button at center of bow.

3. Measure around basket; add 10". Cut several lengths of raffia the determined measurement. Knot raffia around basket.

4. Line basket with excelsior. Place container and bag in basket.

SPEEDY SALSA

*O*ur Quick and Easy Black Bean Salsa would be an enticing appetizer before a holiday meal. Pour the savory salsa into a jar and top off with a decorated lid and a Christmas message. Place the gift in an excelsior-lined clay pot and nestle in a greenery-trimmed wire basket.

QUICK AND EASY BLACK BEAN SALSA

- 1 can (15 ounces) black beans, rinsed and drained
- 1 can (10 ounces) Mexican-style diced tomatoes with lime juice and cilantro
- 1 can (8¾ ounces) whole kernel corn, drained
- ¼ cup finely chopped onion
- 2 teaspoons olive oil
- 2 teaspoons balsamic vinegar
- 1 teaspoon garlic salt
- 1 teaspoon ground cumin
  Tortilla chips to serve

In a medium bowl, combine beans, tomatoes, corn, onion, oil, vinegar, garlic salt, and cumin; stir until well blended. Store in an airtight container in refrigerator 4 hours to let flavors blend. Serve with tortilla chips.

Yield: about 3 cups salsa

SALSA BASKET

You will need a half-pint canning jar with seal and band, red card stock, black permanent fine-point marker, 24" of ⁷/₈"w wired ribbon, craft wire, wire cutters, four artificial holly picks with berries,

4" square wire basket, 4" dia. clay flowerpot, and natural excelsior.

1. For jar lid insert, draw around seal on card stock; cut out. Use marker to write message on insert. Place seal, insert, and band on jar.

2. Tie ribbon into a bow around band.
3. Use wire to attach holly picks to front of basket.
4. Line flowerpot with excelsior. Place flowerpot in basket, then jar in flowerpot.

OLD-FASHIONED FAVORITE

Nothing brings back childhood memories like a favorite candy! Presented in a nostalgic gift bag, our Old-fashioned Peanut Brittle will remind you of Mom's best recipe.

OLD-FASHIONED PEANUT BRITTLE

1½ cups sugar
½ cup light corn syrup
¼ cup water
½ teaspoon salt
1 package (12 ounces) raw Spanish peanuts
1½ tablespoons butter
1 teaspoon baking soda

Butter sides of a heavy large saucepan. Combine sugar, corn syrup, water, and salt in saucepan. Stirring constantly, cook over medium-low heat until sugar dissolves. Using a pastry brush dipped in hot water, wash down any sugar crystals on sides of pan. Attach a candy thermometer to pan, making sure thermometer does not touch bottom of pan. Increase heat to medium and bring to a boil. Cook, without stirring, until mixture reaches 250 degrees (about 6 minutes). Stir in peanuts and continue cooking until mixture reaches hard-crack stage (approximately 300 to 310 degrees). Test about ½ teaspoon mixture in ice water. Mixture will form brittle threads in ice water and will remain brittle when removed from water. Remove from heat and add butter; stir until butter melts. Stir in baking soda (mixture will foam). Pour candy onto a large piece of greased aluminum foil placed on a dampened flat

surface. For thinner brittle, place 1 rubber spatula on top and a second spatula underneath. Lift edges of brittle and stretch as brittle cools. Cool completely. Break into pieces. Store in an airtight container.

Yield: about 1 pound, 12 ounces brittle

DECOUPAGED GIFT BAG

You will need wrapping paper with desired motifs, decoupage glue, brown paper gift bag with handles (we used an 8" x 10" bag), 30" of ⅞"w fabric ribbon,

6" of craft wire, hot glue gun, button, and tissue paper.

1. Cut desired motifs from paper. Follow *Decoupage*, page 152, to apply motifs to front of bag; allow to dry.
2. Use ribbon and follow *Making a Bow*, page 153, to make a bow with two 3" loops, two 5" loops, and two 3½" streamers. Use wire to attach bow to handle of bag. Hot glue button to knot of bow.
3. Line bag with tissue paper; place gift in bag.

PALATE-PLEASING PUDDING

*O**ur Savory Bread Pudding is a sure way to spread joy and warmth throughout the season! An unexpected twist on a holiday classic, the delicious concoction is brimming with the flavors of spices, mushrooms, and Parmesan cheese. It would be great as a side dish with dinner or as a complement to lunch! Package the pudding in an attractive gift bag embellished with a Christmas tree.*

SAVORY BREAD PUDDING

1/4 cup butter or margarine
  2 packages (8 ounces each) fresh mushrooms, sliced
1/2 cup chopped onion
  2 cloves garlic, minced
  1 teaspoon ground black pepper
1 1/2 teaspoons dried Italian herb seasoning, divided
  1 loaf (16 ounces) unsliced French bread, cut into 1-inch cubes (about 10 cups), divided
  7 eggs
  4 cups milk
  1 teaspoon salt
1/2 teaspoon paprika
  1 package (6 ounces) freshly shredded Parmesan cheese

Melt butter in a medium skillet over medium heat. Sauté mushrooms, onion, and garlic until tender (about 5 minutes). Stir in pepper and 1 teaspoon Italian seasoning. Place 2 1/2 cups bread cubes in each of 2 greased 8-inch square baking dishes; top each with mushroom mixture. Cover with remaining bread cubes. In a medium bowl, beat eggs, milk, and salt. Pour milk mixture over bread cubes. In a small bowl, combine paprika, cheese, and remaining 1/2 teaspoon Italian seasoning. Sprinkle over bread mixture. Cover and chill overnight. (*Note:* Casserole can be frozen until ready to bake.) Give with serving instructions.

Yield: about 9 servings in each baking dish

To serve: Store in refrigerator or freezer until ready to bake. Preheat oven to 350 degrees. If chilled, bake uncovered 40 to 50 minutes or until knife inserted in center comes out clean and top is golden brown. Let stand 15 minutes. Cut into 2 1/2-inch squares; serve warm.

If frozen, bake covered 2 hours. Uncover and bake 10 minutes or until knife inserted in center comes out clean and top is golden brown. Let stand 15 minutes. Cut into 2 1/2-inch squares; serve warm.

PUDDING IN A BAG

You will need an 8 1/4" x 13 1/2" brown paper bag, stapler, corrugated craft cardboard, hot glue gun, six 3/8" dia. buttons, two 5/8" dia. self-adhesive hook and loop fasteners, spray adhesive, one 6" x 12" piece each of wrapping paper and card stock, tracing paper, and 9" of 3/8"w satin ribbon.

Use hot glue for all gluing unless otherwise indicated.

1. Leaving front and back uncut, cut away top 4" of sides of bag; staple a 3/4" pleat in each side of bag (Fig. 1).

Fig. 1

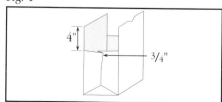

2. Cut a 3/4" x 8 1/4" strip from corrugated cardboard. Glue strip 1/8" from edge on top flap. Fold corners of top flap diagonally to inside (Fig. 2); glue to secure. Glue one button at each end of strip.

Fig. 2

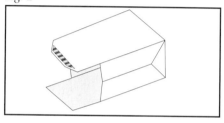

3. Attach two hook and loop fasteners together; apply one fastener under each corner of top flap. Fold top flap over bottom flap; press fasteners to secure.
4. Cut a 7 3/4" x 13" piece from corrugated cardboard. Apply spray adhesive to smooth side of cardboard; smooth onto front of bag.
5. Apply spray adhesive to wrong side of wrapping paper; smooth onto card stock. Trace patterns, page 136, onto tracing paper; cut out. Draw around patterns on wrong side of paper-covered card stock; cut out tree and trunk. Arrange and glue tree and trunk on cardboard. Glue one button at each corner of cardboard.
6. Tie ribbon into a bow; glue bow at base of tree.
7. Place gift in bag.

COOKIE BOUQUET

Who wouldn't love this blossoming surprise! These lemony Flower Cookies, baked on wooden skewer "stems," make a delightful bouquet. Our sponge-painted vase offers a whimsical showcase for the cookies.

FLOWER COOKIES

COOKIES

- 1/2 cup butter or margarine, softened
- 1/2 cup sugar
- 1/2 cup light corn syrup
- 1 egg
- 1 teaspoon lemon extract
- 1/2 teaspoon vanilla extract
- 2 1/2 cups all-purpose flour
- 1/4 teaspoon salt
- 12-inch-long wooden skewers

ICING

- 2 3/4 cups confectioners sugar
- 5 1/2 tablespoons warm water
- 2 1/2 tablespoons meringue powder
- 1 teaspoon lemon extract
- Pink, yellow, and green paste food coloring

For cookies, cream butter and sugar in a large bowl until fluffy. Add corn syrup, egg, and extracts; beat until smooth. In a medium bowl, combine flour and salt. Add dry ingredients to creamed mixture; stir until a soft dough forms. Divide dough into thirds. Wrap in plastic wrap and chill 2 hours or until firm.

Preheat oven to 350 degrees. On a lightly floured surface, use a floured rolling pin to roll out one third of dough to 1/4-inch thickness. Use a knife to cut free-form leaves about 3 inches long and 1 1/4 inches wide. Transfer to a greased baking sheet, allowing space for skewers. Insert 1 inch of a skewer into bottom of each cookie. Bake 7 to 9 minutes or until edges are lightly browned. Cool cookies on baking sheet 2 minutes; transfer to a wire rack to cool completely. Repeat using 2 1/4-inch-wide tulip- and sunflower-shaped cookie cutters to cut out remaining dough. Bake 8 to 10 minutes or until edges are lightly browned. Cool cookies on baking sheet 2 minutes; transfer to a wire rack to cool completely.

For icing, combine confectioners sugar, water, meringue powder, and lemon extract in a medium bowl. Beat at high speed of an electric mixer 7 to 10 minutes or until stiff. Reserve 1/4 cup white icing. Divide remaining icing into 3 small bowls; tint pink, yellow, and green. Adding 1/4 teaspoon water at a time, add enough water to white and tinted icing until icing begins to flow from a spoon. Spoon each icing into a pastry bag fitted with a small round tip. For leaves, pipe outline and fill in with green icing; allow icing surface to harden slightly. Pipe second outline around edge and vein in center with green icing. For tulips, pipe outline and fill in with pink icing. For sunflowers, pipe outline and fill in with yellow icing on half of cookies; allow icing surface to harden slightly. Pipe white dots onto centers of sunflowers. Using yellow and white icing, pipe design onto remaining cookies. Let icing harden. Store in an airtight container.

Yield: about 2 dozen flowers and 1 1/2 dozen leaves

PAINTED FLOWER VASE

You will need glass conditioner cream; clear glass vase (we used a 7 1/2"h vase); 2 1/4"w tulip-shaped cookie cutter; compressed craft sponge; paper towels; yellow, pink, and green Delta Air-Dry PermEnamel™ paints; paintbrushes; and 1 1/2"w wired ribbon.

Refer to Sponge Painting, page 153, before beginning project. Allow paint to dry after each application.

1. Follow manufacturer's instructions to apply conditioner to vase.
2. Draw around cookie cutter on sponge; cut out. Sponge paint three pink tulips around vase. Use paintbrush to paint green stems and leaves on vase, a 3/8"w green line around top of vase, and a yellow wavy line and stripes along bottom of vase. Use end of paintbrush to paint yellow dots on green line and above tulips.
3. Measure around vase; add 12". Cut a length of ribbon the determined measurement. Tie ribbon into a bow around vase.

GARDEN TREASURE

Fresh Garden Pie is overflowing with goodness! This colorful dish — filled with red and green peppers, mushrooms, onion, and cheeses — is great for lunch or a light dinner. Pack the zesty meal in a country-motif pie box to surprise a friend or new neighbor.

FRESH GARDEN PIE

4 cups sliced fresh yellow squash (about 1 pound)

1 package (8 ounces) fresh mushrooms, sliced

1 green pepper, sliced into rings

1 sweet red pepper, sliced into rings

1 onion, sliced and separated into rings

1 clove garlic, minced

1/4 cup olive oil

1 teaspoon salt

1/2 teaspoon ground white pepper

1/8 teaspoon ground red pepper

4 eggs

1/2 cup half and half

1 cup (4 ounces) shredded Gruyère cheese

3/4 cup freshly grated Parmesan cheese

1 unbaked 9-inch pie crust

Preheat oven to 375 degrees. In a large skillet, sauté squash, mushrooms, green pepper, sweet red pepper, onion, and garlic in oil over medium-high heat about 10 minutes or until almost tender. Use a slotted spoon to transfer vegetables to a medium bowl. Sprinkle vegetables with salt, white pepper, and red pepper; stir until well blended. In another medium bowl, beat eggs and half and half until well blended. Stir in cheeses. Pour 2/3 cup egg mixture into crust. Spoon half of vegetables over egg mixture. Continue layering, ending with egg mixture. Bake 35 to 40 minutes or until top is golden brown and filling is set. (If edge of crust browns too quickly, cover with a strip of aluminum foil.) Cool on a wire rack 30 minutes; serve warm. Store in an airtight container in refrigerator.

Yield: about 8 servings

GARDEN PIE BOX

You will need a 9" square x 4"h pie box, wrapping paper, spray adhesive, craft knife, cutting mat, 1 1/2"w wired ribbon, craft wire, wire cutters, colored pencils, black permanent fine-point marker, photocopy of tag design (page 149) on ecru card stock, craft glue stick, colored card stock, hole punch, and 6" of 1/8"w satin ribbon.

1. Unfold box. Cut a piece from wrapping paper 1" larger on all sides than unfolded box. Place wrapping paper right side down on a flat surface.

2. Apply spray adhesive to outside of box. Center unfolded box adhesive side down on paper; press firmly to secure.

3. Use craft knife to cut paper even with edges of box. If box has slits, use craft knife to cut through slits from inside of box.

4. Reassemble box. Place pie in box. Knot a length of wired ribbon around box. Cut a 1 3/4 yd. length of wired ribbon; follow *Making a Bow*, page 153, to make a bow with six 7 1/2" loops and two 9" streamers. Notch streamer ends. Use wire to attach bow to knot of ribbon on box.

5. Use colored pencils to color tag and marker to write message on tag. Cut out tag. Use glue stick to glue tag to colored card stock. Leaving a 1/4" colored card stock border, cut out tag. Punch hole at top center of tag. Use 1/8"w ribbon to attach tag to bow.

HEAT 'N' EAT MEAL

*G*ive the gift of time by preparing your favorite family a scrumptious meal!
*Chicken-Mushroom Lasagna is ready to heat and eat, so it's perfect for busy families
on the go. To carry your offering, make a fabric basket liner and trim the carrier
with silk leaf garland, faux flowers, and sheer ribbon.*

CHICKEN-MUSHROOM LASAGNA

2 cans (10³/₄ ounces each) cream of
     mushroom soup
2 cups milk
¹/₈ teaspoon ground white pepper
1 container (15 ounces) ricotta
     cheese
1 package (10 ounces) frozen
     chopped spinach, thawed
     and squeezed dry
1 egg
1 package (8 ounces) uncooked
     lasagna noodles
1 jar (6 ounces) marinated artichoke
     hearts, drained and coarsely
     chopped
1 jar (4¹/₂ ounces) sliced
     mushrooms, drained
2 cups chopped cooked chicken
2 cups (8 ounces) shredded
     Monterey Jack cheese
¹/₂ cup freshly grated Parmesan cheese

In a medium bowl, combine soup,
milk, and white pepper; stir until well
blended. In another medium bowl,
combine ricotta cheese, spinach, and egg;
stir until well blended. Spoon ¹/₂ cup of
soup mixture over bottom of a greased
9 x 13-inch baking dish. Layer half of
uncooked lasagna noodles over soup
mixture. Layer half of artichoke pieces,
half of mushrooms, 1 cup chicken,
³/₄ cup Monterey Jack cheese, and half of
spinach mixture over noodles. Spoon
2 cups soup mixture over layers. Repeat
layers with remaining lasagna noodles,
artichoke pieces, mushrooms, chicken,
³/₄ cup Monterey Jack cheese, and
spinach mixture. Spoon remaining soup
mixture over layers. Sprinkle top with
Parmesan cheese and remaining ¹/₂ cup
Monterey Jack cheese. Cover and
refrigerate overnight to allow lasagna
noodles to absorb liquids. Give with
serving instructions.

Yield: about 12 servings

To serve: Bake uncovered in a 350-degree
oven 55 to 60 minutes or until golden
brown. Let stand about 15 minutes before
serving. Serve warm.

FABRIC LINER AND TAG

You will need fabric for liner, basket with
handles (we used a 10" x 15" oval
basket), silk leaf garland, hot glue gun,
2"w sheer ribbon, artificial flowers with
leaves, colored pencils, photocopy of tag
design (page 150) on ecru card stock,
and a black permanent fine-point marker.

1. Use fabric and follow *Making a Basket
Liner*, page 152, to make a liner with
unfinished edges large enough to drape
over edges of basket. Place liner in
basket.

2. Measure across front of basket
from handle to handle; add 3". Cut a
length from garland the determined
measurement. Glue center of garland to
center front of basket; glue garland ends
at front of handles. Arrange ribbon along
garland; glue to secure. Glue flowers to
center front of basket.

3. Use colored pencils to color tag. Use
marker to write message on tag. Leaving
a ¹/₄" border, cut out tag.

FROM THE KITCHEN OF:
Jane
Prather

DAINTY DIVINITY

Make sure a little girl's party bubbles over with fun — pass out delicate Orange Divinity in miniature washtubs! Painted with flowers in soft pastels, the party-favor tubs can be used to store trinkets when the fluffy candy is gone.

ORANGE DIVINITY

- 2 egg whites
- 1 package (3 ounces) orange gelatin
- 3 cups sugar
- 3/4 cup hot water
- 3/4 cup light corn syrup

Line a 9-inch square baking pan with aluminum foil, extending foil over 2 sides of pan; grease foil. In a large bowl, use a heavy-duty mixer to beat egg whites until stiff. Gradually beat in dry gelatin until well blended; set aside. Butter sides of a heavy medium saucepan. Combine sugar, hot water, and corn syrup in saucepan. Stirring constantly, cook over medium-low heat until sugar dissolves. Using a pastry brush dipped in hot water, wash down any sugar crystals on sides of pan. Attach a candy thermometer to pan, making sure thermometer does not touch bottom of pan. Increase heat to medium and bring to a boil. Cook, without stirring, until mixture reaches 254 degrees. Test about 1/2 teaspoon mixture in ice water. Mixture will roll into a hard ball in ice water and will remain hard when removed from water. While beating at high speed, slowly pour hot mixture over egg whites; beat until candy thickens and begins to hold its shape (about 4 minutes). Spread into prepared pan; cool completely.

Use ends of foil to lift candy from pan. Cut into 1-inch squares. Store in an airtight container.

Yield: about 5 dozen pieces divinity

WASHTUB FAVORS

For each party favor, you will need light green spray paint; 4" dia. tin washtub with handles; white, yellow, light pink, pink, and green acrylic paint; paintbrush; 1 1/2 yds. of 5/8"w lace; hot glue gun; and one 5" dia. white paper doily.

Allow paint to dry after each application.

1. Spray paint inside and outside of washtub green.
2. Paint top and bottom rims and a 1/4"w band along inside edge of washtub light pink. Paint light pink crisscrossed lines under rim around inside of washtub.
3. Paint pink flowers with light pink highlights; light pink, yellow, and white dots; and green leaves around outside of washtub.
4. Tie lace into a bow; glue bow to rim of washtub. Thread ends of streamers through washtub handles. Line washtub with doily.

TEATIME TANTALIZERS

Our Lemon-Poppy Seed Tea Cakes will brew up some tantalizing conversation when they're delivered in a charming papier-mâché teapot. The simple cookies, made with staples common to your cupboard, are delightful teatime bites.

LEMON-POPPY SEED TEA CAKES

$^1/_2$ cup butter or margarine, softened
1 cup sugar
1 egg
1 tablespoon poppy seed
1 teaspoon lemon extract
1 teaspoon vanilla extract
2 cups all-purpose flour
2 teaspoons baking powder
$^1/_2$ teaspoon salt

In a medium bowl, cream butter and sugar until fluffy. Add egg, poppy seed, and extracts; beat until smooth. In a small bowl, combine flour, baking powder, and salt. Add dry ingredients to creamed mixture; stir until a soft dough forms. Divide dough into fourths. Wrap in plastic wrap and chill 1 hour or until firm.

Preheat oven to 400 degrees. On a lightly floured surface, use a floured rolling pin to roll out one fourth of dough to $^1/_8$-inch thickness. Use a 1$^3/_4$-inch-diameter fluted-edge cookie cutter to cut out cookies. Place 2 inches apart on a lightly greased baking sheet. Bake 4 to 6 minutes or until edges are lightly browned. Transfer cookies to a wire rack to cool. Repeat with remaining dough. Store in an airtight container.

Yield: about 8 dozen cookies

DECOUPAGED TEAPOT

You will need green acrylic paint, paintbrush, papier-mâché teapot, floral-motif wrapping paper, decoupage glue, foam brush, clear acrylic spray sealer, gold fine-point paint pen, pink colored pencil, black permanent fine-point marker, photocopy of tag design (page 149) on green card stock, decorative-edge craft scissors, hole punch, and 12" of $^1/_8$"w satin ribbon.

Allow paint, glue, sealer, and paint pen to dry after each application.

1. Paint outside of lid and teapot green.
2. Use wrapping paper and follow *Decoupage,* page 152, to apply floral motifs to teapot.
3. Use paint pen to add details and outline motifs on teapot.
4. Use colored pencil to color heart and marker to write message on tag. Leaving a $^1/_4$" border, use craft scissors to cut out tag. Punch hole in corner of tag. Use ribbon to attach tag to teapot.

SIMPLY IRRESISTIBLE

*Share a little slice of heaven with a decadent Chocolate-Mocha Cake.
Its rich flavor comes from a "secret" ingredient — strongly brewed coffee!
Cover a cake box in wrapping paper to package the dessert and finish
with a button-centered bow and a coordinating gift tag.*

CHOCOLATE-MOCHA CAKES

CAKES

- 2 cups all-purpose flour
- 2 cups sugar
- 1 teaspoon baking soda
- $1/4$ teaspoon salt
- 1 cup butter or margarine
- 1 cup strongly brewed coffee
- $1/4$ cup cocoa
- $1/2$ cup buttermilk
- 2 eggs
- 1 teaspoon vanilla extract

ICING

- $1/2$ cup butter or margarine
- $1/3$ cup strongly brewed coffee
- $1/4$ cup cocoa
- 1 package (16 ounces) confectioners sugar
- 1 teaspoon vanilla extract
- 1 cup chopped pecans, toasted

Preheat oven to 350 degrees. Cover two $8^{1}/_{2}$-inch square pieces of cardboard with freezer paper or plastic wrap. Line bottoms of two 8-inch square cake pans with waxed paper; grease waxed paper.

For cakes, combine flour, sugar, baking soda, and salt in a large bowl. In a medium saucepan, combine butter, coffee, and cocoa. Stirring constantly, bring to a boil over medium-high heat. Beat coffee mixture into dry ingredients until well blended. Beat in buttermilk, eggs, and vanilla. Pour batter into prepared pans. Bake 27 to 30 minutes or until a toothpick inserted in center of cake comes out clean. Cool in pans 10 minutes. Remove from pans and cool completely on a wire rack. Place cakes on prepared cardboard pieces.

For icing, combine butter, coffee, and cocoa in a small saucepan. Stirring constantly, bring to a boil over medium-high heat. Transfer to a heat-resistant large bowl. Beat in confectioners sugar and vanilla until mixture is smooth. Stir in pecans. Spread icing over cakes. Store in an airtight container.

Yield: 2 cakes, about 8 servings each

COVERED BOX AND TAG

You will need a 9" x 9" x 4"h cake box, wrapping paper, spray adhesive, craft knife, cutting mat, 1 yd. of $1/2$"w wired ribbon, hot glue gun, $1^{1}/_{8}$" dia. button, colored pencils, black permanent fine-point marker, photocopy of tag design (page 150) on ecru card stock, and a $3^{1}/_{2}$" long craft pick.

1. Unfold box. Cut a piece from wrapping paper 1" larger on all sides than unfolded box. Place wrapping paper right side down on a flat surface. Apply spray adhesive to outside of box. Center unfolded box adhesive side down on paper; press firmly to secure.
2. Use craft knife to cut paper even with edges of box. If box has slits, use craft knife to cut through slits from inside of box.
3. Reassemble box. Place cake in box.
4. Use ribbon and follow *Making a Bow*, page 153, to make a bow with four 6" loops and two 5" streamers. Glue bow to box. Glue button to center of bow.
5. Use colored pencils to color and marker to write message on tag. Leaving a $1/8$" border, cut out tag. Glue craft pick to back of tag. Insert pick in knot of bow.

AN APPLE FOR THE TEACHER

*D*on't send your child to school with an ordinary apple for the teacher! Stir up a batch
of easy-to-make Apple-Orange Butter. Tucked with a can of biscuits in a flowerpot rimmed with
dried apple slices, the fruity spread will earn your child top honors for creativity.

APPLE-ORANGE BUTTER

2 cans (11 ounces each) mandarin
   oranges in light syrup, undrained
1 package (6 ounces) dried apples,
   chopped
2 cups sugar
$1/2$ cup orange juice
2 tablespoons freshly squeezed lemon
   juice
1 teaspoon ground ginger
$1/4$ teaspoon ground allspice
1 can (12 ounces) biscuits to serve

In a heavy large saucepan, combine
oranges, apples, sugar, orange juice,
lemon juice, ginger, and allspice. Stirring
frequently, cook over medium heat until
apples are tender and mixture thickens
(about 30 minutes). Process in a food
processor until smooth. Store in an
airtight container in refrigerator.
Give with can of biscuits.

Yield: about $3^{1/2}$ cups fruit butter

TEACHER'S GIFT ENSEMBLE

You will need white, blue, and brown
acrylic paint; paintbrushes; $6^{1/2}$" dia.
terra-cotta flowerpot; toothbrush; paper
towel; clear matte varnish; hot glue gun;
dried apple slices; natural raffia; fabric;
decorative-edge craft scissors; kraft
paper; black permanent fine-point
marker; spray adhesive; red shredded
paper; pinking shears; blue card stock;
hole punch; and a jar with an airtight lid
to fit in flowerpot (we used a half-pint jar
with hinged lid).

*Refer to Spatter Painting, page 153,
before beginning project. Allow paint
and varnish to dry after each
application. Use hot glue for all gluing
unless otherwise indicated. Refrigerate
butter and biscuits until ready to
present gift.*

1. Paint inside of flowerpot and outside
rim white. Spatter paint white areas
brown. Paint outside of flowerpot under
rim blue. Spatter paint blue area white.
Apply two to three coats of varnish to
entire flowerpot.
2. Glue apple slices around rim of
flowerpot. Knot several 24" lengths of
raffia around flowerpot under rim.
3. For label, cut a $2^{7/8}$" x $3^{1/4}$" piece from
fabric. Use craft scissors to cut a
$2^{1/4}$" x $2^{1/2}$" piece from kraft paper. Use
marker to write message and draw
"stitches" along edges of kraft paper
piece. Apply spray adhesive to wrong
side of fabric and kraft paper. Smooth
fabric onto flowerpot, then kraft paper

onto fabric. Line flowerpot with
shredded paper.
4. For biscuit bag, cut an 8" x 24" piece
from fabric. Use fabric and follow *Making
a Fabric Bag*, page 154, to make a bag
with square corners. Use pinking shears
to trim top of bag. Place can of biscuits
(from recipe this page) in bag. Knot
several 12" lengths of raffia around top of
bag. Glue one dried apple slice to knot of
raffia. Tie several 10" lengths of raffia into
a bow; glue bow to apple slice.
5. For biscuit tag, cut a $1^{3/4}$" square from
card stock. Spatter paint tag white. Use
craft scissors to cut a $1^{1/2}$" square from
kraft paper. Use glue stick to glue kraft
paper to card stock. Use marker to write
message and draw "stitches" along edges
of tag. Punch a hole in corner of tag. Use
raffia to attach tag to bag.
6. To embellish jar, measure around jar
lid; add 10". Cut several lengths of raffia
the determined measurement; knot
around jar lid.
7. For jar tag, cut a $2^{5/8}$" x 4" piece from
card stock. Matching short edges, fold
card stock in half. Spatter paint outside of
card stock white. Use craft scissors to cut
a $1^{3/4}$" x $2^{3/8}$" piece from kraft paper.
Apply spray adhesive to wrong side of
kraft paper; smooth onto card stock. Use
marker to write message and draw
"stitches" along edges of tag. Punch hole
in corner of tag. Use raffia to attach tag
to jar.
8. Place bag and jar in flowerpot.

AUTUMN OFFERING

*A*utumn brings falling leaves, bright blue skies, chilly
afternoons…and our Nutty Brown Sugar Bars! Pack the layered delights
in a sponge-painted tin and finish the gift with a wired-ribbon bow.

NUTTY BROWN SUGAR BARS

FILLING

- 1/2 cup butter or margarine
- 1/2 cup firmly packed brown sugar
- 1/2 cup evaporated milk
- 1 cup graham cracker crumbs
- 1 cup flaked coconut
- 1/2 cup chopped pecans
- 15 graham crackers (2 1/2 x 5 inches each)

ICING

- 1 cup firmly packed brown sugar
- 3 tablespoons evaporated milk
- 2 tablespoons butter or margarine
- 1 cup confectioners sugar
- 1 teaspoon vanilla extract

For filling, combine butter, brown sugar, and evaporated milk in a heavy medium saucepan. Stirring constantly over medium-high heat, bring to a boil and boil 1 minute. Remove from heat. Stir in cracker crumbs, coconut, and pecans. Line bottom of a 9 x 13-inch baking pan with half of graham crackers. Pour filling over crackers. Cover filling with remaining graham crackers, pressing to make crackers level.

For icing, combine brown sugar, evaporated milk, and butter in a heavy medium saucepan. Stirring constantly over medium-high heat, cook until mixture begins to boil (about 3 minutes). Remove from heat. Add confectioners sugar and vanilla; stir until smooth. Quickly spread icing over graham crackers. Cool in pan. Cut into 1 x 2-inch bars. Store in an airtight container.

Yield: about 4 dozen bars

SPONGE-PAINTED TIN

You will need spray primer, 10" dia. tin with lid, peach spray paint, tracing paper, compressed craft sponge, yellow and copper acrylic paint, glossy wood-tone spray, 1 1/2 yds. of 1 1/2"w wired ribbon, two 18" lengths of 3/8"w satin ribbon, and a hot glue gun.

Refer to Sponge Painting, page 153, before beginning project. Allow primer, paint, and wood-tone spray to dry after each application.

1. Apply primer to outside of lid and tin. Spray paint outside of lid and tin peach.
2. Trace pattern, page 145, onto tracing paper; cut out. Draw around pattern on sponge; cut out.
3. Sponge paint yellow and copper leaves on tin and lid. Lightly apply wood-tone spray to lid and tin.
4. Tie wired ribbon into a bow around tin. Tie satin ribbon lengths together into a bow; glue to knot of wired ribbon bow. Trim ends of ribbons.

CHARMING CHUTNEY

*S*weet, tangy, and spicy all in one! This chunky Pineapple Chutney makes a great topper for cream cheese and crackers, and it adds zip to meats. Create country baskets by wrapping with button-embellished fabric and padding with fiberfill. Place jars of the mouth-watering chutney inside and add photocopied gift tags for a charming "hello."

PINEAPPLE CHUTNEY

- 3 cans (15¼ ounces each) pineapple tidbits in juice, drained
- 3 cups chopped onions
- 3 cups sugar
- 2 cups golden raisins
- 1 cup apple cider vinegar
- 1 cup chopped sweet yellow pepper
- 1 tablespoon grated lemon zest
- 1 tablespoon freshly squeezed lemon juice
- 2 teaspoons salt
- 2 teaspoons mustard seed
- 2 teaspoons celery seed
- ½ teaspoon ground turmeric

In a Dutch oven, combine pineapple, onions, sugar, raisins, vinegar, yellow pepper, lemon zest, lemon juice, salt, mustard seed, celery seed, and turmeric. Stirring constantly, bring mixture to a boil over medium-high heat. Reduce heat to medium low. Stirring occasionally, simmer uncovered 50 to 60 minutes or until thickened. Spoon into heat-resistant jars; cover and cool to room temperature. Store in refrigerator. Serve over cream cheese with crackers or as a condiment.

Yield: about 6½ cups chutney

BUTTON BASKETS

For each basket, you will need a half-pint canning jar, seal, and band; fabric for jar lid and to cover basket; poster board; spray adhesive; basket (we used a 3¼" dia. x 3"h basket with handle); string; fabric marking pen; thumbtack; rubber band; polyester fiberfill; assorted buttons; green embroidery floss; 1"w wired ribbon; natural excelsior; colored pencils; photocopy of tag design (page 150) on ecru card stock; and a black permanent fine-point marker.

1. Draw around seal on wrong side of fabric and poster board; cut out circles. Apply spray adhesive to wrong side of fabric circle; smooth fabric circle onto poster board circle. Place gift in jar; place seal on jar. Position poster board circle on seal; twist band onto jar.

2. Measure width of basket from rim to rim (Fig. 1); add 4". Cut a square from fabric the determined measurement.

Fig. 1

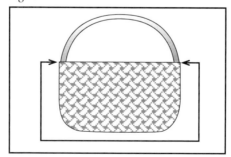

3. Matching right sides, fold fabric square in half from top to bottom and again from left to right. Tie one end of string to pen. Measure one half of the determined measurement from pen; insert thumbtack through string at this point. Insert thumbtack through fabric and keeping string taut, mark cutting line (Fig. 2).

Cutting through all layers, cut out circle along drawn line.

Fig. 2

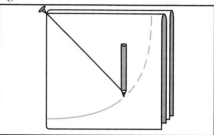

4. Place basket at center of wrong side of fabric circle. Gather circle around rim of basket; secure with rubber band. Place fiberfill between basket and fabric.

5. Sew buttons on fabric. Use floss and refer to *Embroidery Stitches*, page 152, to work *Running Stitches* for stems and *Lazy Daisy Stitches* for leaves under buttons as desired.

6. Measure around rim of basket; add 16". Cut a length of ribbon the determined measurement. Tie ribbon into a bow around rim, covering rubber band.

7. Line basket with excelsior; place jar in basket.

8. Use colored pencils to color tag and marker to write message on tag. Cut out tag. Place tag in basket.

"I LOVE CHOCOLATE!"

Here's something to love! Our velvety Fudge Brownies are chock-full of crunchy pecans and covered with rich whipped icing. Present the sweet surprise in a basket designed just for chocolate lovers. A ribbon bow and painted wooden heart complete your fudgy greeting.

FUDGE BROWNIES

BROWNIES

    1 cup butter or margarine
    4 ounces unsweetened baking
         chocolate, chopped
    2 cups sugar
    4 eggs
    2 teaspoons vanilla extract
 1 1/4 cups all-purpose flour
    1 cup chopped pecans

ICING

    4 ounces unsweetened baking
         chocolate, chopped
  1/3 cup butter or margarine
 2 1/2 cups confectioners sugar
  1/2 cup whipping cream
    1 teaspoon vanilla extract

Preheat oven to 350 degrees. For brownies, place butter and chocolate in a large microwave-safe bowl. Microwave on medium power (50%) until mixture melts, stirring after each minute. Stir in sugar. Allow mixture to cool 10 minutes. Beat in eggs, 1 at a time, and vanilla. Stir in flour and pecans. Pour mixture into 2 greased 8-inch square aluminum foil pans. Bake 15 to 20 minutes or until edges begin to pull away from sides of pan. Cool on a wire rack.

For icing, place chocolate and butter in a small microwave-safe bowl. Microwave on medium power (50%) until mixture melts, stirring after each minute. Cool to room temperature. In a medium bowl, combine confectioners sugar, whipping cream, and vanilla; beat until smooth. Add cooled chocolate mixture and beat until well blended. Spread icing over brownies. Chill about 1 hour or until firm enough to cut.

Cut into 2-inch squares. Store in an airtight container in refrigerator. Serve at room temperature.

Yield: about 16 brownies each pan

"I LOVE CHOCOLATE" BASKET

You will need fabric, tracing paper, transfer paper, 10 1/4" square basket with rim at least 3/4"w, red acrylic paint, paintbrush, 4" high unfinished wooden heart, black permanent fine-point marker, 1 1/2 yds of 5/8"w brown grosgrain ribbon, 8" of craft wire, 24" square of clear cellophane, and a hot glue gun.

1. Use fabric and follow *Making a Basket Liner*, page 152, to make a liner with unfinished edges.

2. Trace pattern, page 138, onto tracing paper. Use transfer paper to transfer pattern to rim of basket. Paint heart on rim and wooden heart red; allow to dry. Use marker to draw over words, outline heart on rim, draw border along edges, and write message on wooden heart.

3. Use ribbon and follow *Making a Bow*, page 153, to make a bow with two 6 1/2" loops, two 6" loops, two 5" loops, and two 7" streamers.

4. Center gift on cellophane. Gather cellophane over gift; use wire on bow to secure gathers. Glue wooden heart to center of bow.

5. Place liner and gift in basket.

SASSY SALSA!

*R*ing in the festivities of
*Cinco de Mayo with our Easy Sassy
Salsa! Tortilla chips are the perfect
partner for the flavorful dip, and
a cute felt sombrero tops the jar
for a celebratory finish.*

EASY SASSY SALSA

  1 can (14$^{1}/_{2}$ ounces) Mexican-style
      stewed tomatoes, undrained
  1 can (10 ounces) diced tomatoes
      and green chiles, undrained
  1 can (4$^{1}/_{2}$ ounces) chopped green
      chiles, undrained
$^{1}/_{2}$ cup chopped fresh cilantro
  2 tablespoons dried minced onion
  2 teaspoons ground cumin
1$^{1}/_{2}$ teaspoons garlic salt
  1 teaspoon garlic powder
      Tortilla chips to serve

Combine first 3 ingredients in a food
processor or blender. Add cilantro, onion,
cumin, garlic salt, and garlic powder.
Pulse process until well blended. Transfer
into an airtight container and chill
4 hours to let flavors blend. Serve with
tortilla chips.

Yield: about 3$^{1}/_{2}$ cups salsa

SOMBRERO JAR TOPPER

You will need a 6" dia. felt witch's hat
with a 2$^{3}/_{4}$" dia. opening, embroidery
floss, ironing board, steam iron, hot glue
gun, $^{3}/_{8}$"w decorative cord, nine 10mm
pom-poms, and a jar with a 2$^{3}/_{4}$" dia. lid.

1. Turn hat wrong side out. Tie a 3" length
of floss tightly around hat $^{1}/_{2}$" from tip; tie
ends together to secure. Turn hat right
side out.

2. To curl hat brim, place center of hat
brim against edge of pointed end of
ironing board; press using steam iron set
at medium-high heat. Rotate and press
until entire brim is curled.

3. Trimming to fit, glue cord around hat
for hatband and outer edge of hat brim.
4. Sew pom-poms to cord at 2" intervals
around outer edge of hat brim.
5. Place hat on jar.

LITTLE ITALY

*S*hare a little taste of Italy with a gift of robust homemade Bruschetta — slices of warm garlic bread topped with a Mediterranean-style salsa. Slip a loaf of French bread into a crafty painted bag and present it with a jar of the topping. Your friends can toast their own mouth-watering appetizers.

BRUSCHETTA

- 3 large cloves garlic, minced
- 2 tablespoons olive oil
- 4 cups peeled, seeded, and chopped Roma tomatoes (about 2¼ pounds)
- 2 tablespoons balsamic vinegar
- 2 tablespoons chopped fresh basil leaves
- ½ teaspoon ground black pepper
- ½ teaspoon salt
- 1 baguette French bread (10 ounces and about 2½ inches in diameter) to serve

In a large saucepan, sauté garlic in oil over medium heat about 2 minutes or until garlic begins to brown. Stir in tomatoes and vinegar. Stirring frequently, cook about 20 minutes or until mixture thickens and volume reduces by half. Stir in basil, pepper, and salt. Store in an airtight container in refrigerator. Give with bread and serving instructions.

Yield: about 2 cups topping

To serve: Cut bread into ½-inch-thick slices. Toast bread slices under broiler about 1 minute on each side. Brush top of each slice with olive oil. Place 1½ to 2 teaspoons topping on each slice; broil about 3 minutes or until heated through. Serve immediately.

Yield: about 38 appetizers

TOMATO AND OLIVE BAG AND JAR

You will need tracing paper; compressed craft sponges; white, red, green, dark green, and black acrylic paint; canvas bag with drawstrings (we used a 6" x 17½" canvas bag); paintbrush; quart jar with seal and band; muslin; ³/8"w grosgrain ribbon; hot glue gun; craft glue, decorative-edge craft scissors; photocopy of tag design (page 146) on tan card stock; 2" x 3" piece of red corrugated craft cardboard; hole punch; and a black permanent fine-point marker.

Refer to Sponge Painting, page 153, before beginning project. Allow paint and craft glue to dry after each application. Use craft glue for all gluing unless otherwise indicated.

1. Trace patterns, page 146, onto tracing paper; cut out. Using patterns, cut square, tomato, olive, and tomato stem shapes from sponges.
2. Sponge paint evenly spaced black squares along long edges of bag. Sponge paint red tomatoes, dark green and black olives, and dark green tomato stems on bag. Lightly sponge paint green highlights on each dark green olive.
3. Paint green detail lines on tomato stems and dark green vines on bag.
4. Use end of paintbrush to paint white dots on black squares and black olives and red dots on green olives.
5. For jar lid cover, draw around seal on muslin; cut out along drawn line. Sponge paint one black and two dark green olives on muslin. Lightly sponge paint green highlights on each dark green olive. Use end of paintbrush to paint a white dot on black olive and red dots on green olives. Paint green vines on muslin. Place seal, then jar lid cover on jar. Twist band onto jar.
6. Measure around jar band; cut a length of ribbon the determined measurement. Hot glue ribbon around jar band. For bow, cut one ³/4", one 3", and one 4" length from ribbon. For streamers, fold 4" ribbon length in half; glue fold over ribbon seam on jar band. Overlap and glue ends of 3" ribbon to form loop. Flatten loop with seam at back. Overlapping ends at back, wrap ³/4" ribbon length around center of loop; glue to secure. Glue bow over fold on streamers.
7. Use craft scissors to cut out tag. Use glue stick to glue tag to cardboard. Punch hole in corner of tag. Place bread in bag. Thread tag onto drawstring on bag; knot drawstring ends together to secure.

Bruschetta

TOUCHDOWN TREATS

*A*ny football fanatic will love settling in for the big game
with our zesty Caesar Snack Mix. The crunchy snack is certain to
score a touchdown! You'll be a real team player when you pack
the mix in an appliquéd football-theme bag.

CAESAR SNACK MIX

    1 package (14 ounces) oyster
       crackers
    1 package (7 ounces) rye chip
       crackers
    2 packages (6 ounces each) plain
       croutons
    1 package (3¼ ounces) pencil-size
       plain bread sticks, broken into
       1-inch pieces
    ½ cup olive oil
    ½ cup butter or margarine, melted
    ½ cup freshly grated Parmesan cheese
    6 tablespoons freshly squeezed
       lemon juice
    6 cloves garlic, minced
    2 tablespoons Dijon-style mustard
    2 tablespoons white wine
       Worcestershire sauce
    2 tablespoons parsley flakes
    ½ teaspoon salt
    ½ teaspoon ground white pepper

Preheat oven to 250 degrees. Place
crackers, croutons, and bread stick pieces
in a large roasting pan. In a medium bowl,
whisk oil, melted butter, Parmesan cheese,
lemon juice, garlic, mustard, white wine
Worcestershire sauce, parsley, salt, and
white pepper until well blended. Pour over
cracker mixture; toss until well coated.
Bake 1 hour, stirring every 15 minutes.
Spread on aluminum foil to cool. Store in
an airtight container.

Yield: about 20 cups snack mix

FOOTBALL BAG

You will need paper-backed fusible web,
green fabric, 12" x 15" canvas bag with
attached bag tie, 1⅔ yds. of ¼"w and
1 yd. of ⅜"w white grosgrain ribbon,
¼"w and ⅜"w fusible web tape, white
and brown felt, black permanent fine-
point and medium-point markers, tracing
paper, two colors of card stock, craft glue
stick, craft knife, cutting mat, and two
1 yd. lengths each of two coordinating
colors of ⅜"w curling ribbon.

1. Cut one 6" x 10⅞" piece each from
web and fabric. For football field, fuse
web to wrong side of green fabric; fuse
green fabric to bag ¼" from side and
bottom edges of bag. Cut ¼"w ribbon into
ten 6" lengths. Cut ⅜"w ribbon into two
6¾" lengths and two 11" lengths. Fuse
web tape to one side of each grosgrain
ribbon length.
2. Beginning ¾" from one short edge of
field, fuse 6" ribbon lengths evenly across
field. Overlapping as necessary, fuse 11"
ribbon lengths along top and bottom
edges and 6¾" ribbon lengths along side
edges of field.
3. Use patterns, page 147, and follow
Making Appliqués, page 152, to make
one football appliqué from brown felt
and two stripe appliqués from white felt.
Fuse football to field. Use medium-point
marker to draw seams and laces on
football. Arrange and fuse stripes
on football.
4. For tag, trace small and large triangle
patterns, page 147, onto tracing paper;
cut out. Draw around small triangle on
one color of card stock. Draw around
large triangle on remaining card stock.
Cut triangles out. Glue small triangle to
large triangle. Use fine-point marker to
write message on tag. Use craft knife to
cut a ½" vertical slit in top corner of tag;
thread tag onto bag ties.
5. Place gift in bag. Tie bag ties into a
bow around top of bag. Tie curling
ribbons together into a bow around top
of bag; curl ribbon ends.

HAPPY NEW YEAR!

On New Year's Eve, start the fireworks early by presenting a bottle of Spicy Red Wine. The spirited drink is easy to make by infusing a bottle of red wine with fruit and spices. Our sparkler-inspired bottle sleeve will add to the evening's festivities.

SPICY RED WINE

Best if wine is used within 1 week.

    6 cinnamon sticks, broken
         into pieces
    6 whole cloves
    6 whole allspice
    2 cups water
    1 cup sugar
    2 lemons, sliced
    2 oranges, sliced
    1 bottle (1.5 liters) red wine

Place cinnamon sticks, cloves, and allspice in a small square of cheesecloth; tie with kitchen string. In a non-aluminum Dutch oven, combine water, sugar, lemon slices, and orange slices. Stirring occasionally, cook over medium-low heat until sugar dissolves. Add spice bundle and wine; cook 5 minutes. Transfer mixture to a heatproof glass container. Let stand at room temperature overnight to let flavors blend.

Strain wine into a gift bottle. Store in refrigerator. Serve chilled or at room temperature.

Yield: about 8 cups wine

NEW YEAR'S BOTTLE SLEEVE

You will need a bottle with spigot, poster board, masking tape, drawing compass, craft knife, cutting mat, hot glue gun, blue spray paint, tracing paper, transfer paper, gold paint pen, gold glitter dimensional paint, gold acrylic paint, toothbrush, paper towel, and one each gold and blue metallic party sprays with stars.

Allow spray paint, paint pen, and dimensional paint to dry after each application.

1. For bottle sleeve, measure height of bottle from top to bottom. Measure around bottle; add 1". Cut a piece from poster board the determined measurements.
2. Overlapping long edges 1", use tape to secure inside and outside edges at back of sleeve.
3. Cut a slit at center front bottom of sleeve; trim to fit around spigot.
4. Draw around opposite end of sleeve on poster board; cut out circle top just outside drawn line. Use compass to draw a 1½" small circle at center of circle top. Use craft knife to cut out small circle and a ½"w slit at edge of circle top. Aligning slit in circle top at center front of sleeve, glue circle top inside sleeve ¼" below top edge.
5. Spray paint sleeve blue.
6. Trace design, page 144, onto tracing paper. Use transfer paper to transfer design to center front of sleeve. Use paint pen to draw over design. Use dimensional paint to paint over gold painted dots. Follow *Spatter Painting,* page 153, to lightly spatter paint sleeve gold; allow to dry.
7. Insert ends of sprays through slit in top; use tape to secure ends of sprays inside sleeve. Place sleeve over bottle.

CHOCOLATE DELIGHTS

*T*hese sophisticated Triple *Chocolate Truffles will delight even the pickiest chocolate lover! Displayed in beribboned gift boxes, the rich candies are sure to cause a stir when given as birthday party favors.*

TRIPLE CHOCOLATE TRUFFLES

- 3 cups semisweet chocolate chips
- 1 can (14 ounces) chocolate sweetened condensed milk
- 3½ cups chopped pecans, toasted, coarsely ground, and divided
- 3 tablespoons chocolate-flavored liqueur
- 1 teaspoon vanilla extract

In a medium saucepan, combine chocolate chips and chocolate sweetened condensed milk. Stirring constantly, cook over low heat until chocolate chips melt and mixture is smooth. Stir in 1 cup ground pecans, liqueur, and vanilla until well blended. Remove from heat and transfer to a medium bowl. Cover and chill 2 hours or until firm.

Shape mixture into 1-inch balls; roll in remaining ground pecans. Store in an airtight container in refrigerator.

Yield: about 6 dozen truffles

FLOWERED GIFT BOXES

For each box, you will need a 1½" x 1⅜" x 10" gift box with clear plastic lid, 1 yd. of 1⅜"w sheer ribbon, hot glue gun, and a silk flower pick.

Place gift in box. Tie ribbon into a bow around box. Position streamers as desired; spot glue to secure. Glue pick to knot of bow.

HEARTFELT VALENTINE

You're sure to win the heart of someone dear with an incredibly moist Chocolate-Coconut-Rum Cake. Show off the decadent dessert in a heart-shaped pan embellished with lace, fabric, and a decorative tag.

CHOCOLATE-COCONUT-RUM CAKES

For your special gifts, you will need cake pans with plastic lids because the lids will be decorated.

CAKES

- 1 package (18¼ ounces) devil's food cake mix
- 1 package (3.9 ounces) chocolate instant pudding mix
- 4 eggs
- ½ cup water
- ½ cup vegetable oil
- ½ cup dark rum
- 4 ounces white baking chocolate, finely chopped

ICING

- 3 tablespoons milk
- 2 ounces white baking chocolate
- 3 tablespoons dark rum
- ¾ cup butter or margarine, softened
- 1 cup confectioners sugar
- 1½ cups flaked coconut

Preheat oven to 350 degrees. For cakes, combine cake mix, pudding mix, eggs, water, oil, and rum in a large bowl; beat until well blended. Stir in chocolate. Pour into 2 lightly greased 9-inch heart-shaped aluminum foil pans. Bake 25 to 30 minutes or until a toothpick inserted in center of cake comes out clean. Cool in pans.

For icing, combine milk and chocolate in a small saucepan. Stirring constantly, cook over low heat until mixture is smooth. Remove from heat; stir in rum. Transfer mixture to a heatproof bowl. Refrigerate about 15 minutes or until cool.

In a medium bowl, beat butter and confectioners sugar until fluffy (about 3 minutes). Gradually beat in cooled chocolate mixture. Spread over cooled cakes. Sprinkle tops with coconut. Cover cakes with plastic lids. Store at room temperature.

Yield: two 9-inch heart-shaped cakes, 8 to 10 servings each cake

DECORATED CAKE PAN

You will need paper-backed fusible web, fabric, poster board, craft knife, cutting mat, craft glue, hot glue gun, ⅝"w flat lace, 27" of 6"w tulle, tracing paper, decorative-edge craft scissors, 7" of ⅛"w satin ribbon, and a black permanent fine-point marker.

Use hot glue for all gluing unless otherwise indicated.

1. Draw around top of lid of heart-shaped pan (from recipe this page) on wrong side of web. Fuse web to wrong side of fabric. Cut out heart ¼" inside drawn line. Fuse heart to poster board; cut out along edges of fabric. For border, measure ⅝" from edge of heart; use craft knife to cut out center of heart. Set aside cutout piece for tag.
2. Use craft glue to glue border to lid; allow to dry. Glue lace along outer edge of heart.
3. Tie tulle into a bow; glue bow at top of border.
4. Cut a 3¼" x 4" tag from fabric-covered poster board set aside in Step 1. Trimming to fit and mitering corners as necessary, glue lace along edges of tag.
5. Trace pattern, page 147, onto tracing paper; cut out. Draw around pattern on poster board; use craft scissors to cut out. Use craft glue to glue heart to tag. Tie ribbon into a bow; glue to heart. Use marker to write message on tag.

SWEET NOTHINGS

*E*xpress your affection with these conversation-piece cookies! The recipe makes enough "sweet nothings" to share with lots of loved ones. Pack trios of the cookies in wrapping paper-covered folders topped with doilies, ribbon, and silk flowers.

"I LOVE YOU" COOKIES

COOKIES

- 3/4 cup butter or margarine, softened
- 1 cup confectioners sugar
- 1 egg
- 2 teaspoons vanilla extract
- 2 1/2 cups all-purpose flour
- 1/4 teaspoon salt

ICING

- 1/3 cup water
- 2 tablespoons plus 2 teaspoons light corn syrup
- 5 1/3 cups confectioners sugar
- 3 to 3 1/2 teaspoons half and half
- 1 1/2 teaspoons vanilla extract
- Red paste food coloring

For cookies, cream butter and confectioners sugar in a large bowl until fluffy. Add egg and vanilla; beat until smooth. In a medium bowl, combine flour and salt. Add dry ingredients to creamed mixture; stir until a soft dough forms. Divide dough in half. Wrap in plastic wrap and chill 1 hour.

Preheat oven to 350 degrees. On a lightly floured surface, use a floured rolling pin to roll out half of dough to 1/4-inch thickness. Use 2-inch-high "I" and "U" alphabet cookie cutters to cut out about 10 cookies of each letter. Use a 2 1/4-inch-wide heart-shaped cookie cutter to cut out about 10 heart cookies. Transfer to a greased baking sheet. Bake 8 to 10 minutes or until bottoms are lightly browned. Transfer to a wire rack with waxed paper underneath to cool. Repeat with remaining dough.

For icing, combine water and corn syrup in a heavy medium saucepan. Add confectioners sugar; stir until well blended. Using a pastry brush dipped in hot water, wash down any sugar crystals on sides of pan. Attach a candy thermometer to pan, making sure thermometer does not touch bottom of pan. Stirring constantly, cook over medium heat until mixture reaches 100 degrees. Remove from heat; stir in half and half and vanilla. Cool icing 5 minutes. Transfer 1 cup icing to a small bowl; tint red. Spoon red icing over heart cookies. (Reuse icing on waxed paper if necessary. If icing becomes too thick, thin with water, a few drops at a time.) Reserving a small amount of icing for Step 3 of Cookie Folders, spoon white icing over letter cookies. Let icing harden. Store in a single layer in an airtight container.

Yield: about 20 sets of cookies

COOKIE FOLDERS

For each folder, you will need 2 3/4"w white paper lace, decorative-edge craft scissors, red-and-white checked wrapping paper, spray adhesive, 5 3/4" x 8 1/4" piece of red card stock, ruler, icing (from recipe this page), 2 3/4" x 5 1/2" piece of white plastic foam tray, clear plastic wrap, transparent tape, craft glue, 7/8"w red wired ribbon, hot glue gun, and an artificial flower.

1. For outside of folder, cut a 7" length from paper lace. Use craft scissors to cut a 5 1/2" x 8" piece from wrapping paper. Apply spray adhesive to wrong side of wrapping paper; center and smooth onto card stock. Apply spray adhesive to wrong side of paper lace; center and smooth onto wrapping paper.

2. For inside of folder, refer to Fig. 1 and use ruler and one point of scissors to score card stock. Use craft scissors to cut two 1" x 5 1/4" pieces from wrapping paper. Apply spray adhesive to wrong side of each piece; center and smooth onto top and bottom flaps of folder.

Fig. 1

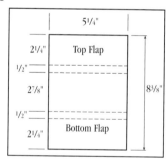

3. Use a small amount of icing to secure cookies on tray. Wrap plastic wrap tightly around tray, overlapping edges on bottom; secure with tape. Use craft glue to glue tray to center section of folder; allow to dry.

4. Overlapping as necessary and folding along scored lines, fold folder; secure with tape.

5. Cut one 8" and one 11" length of ribbon. Overlapping ends at top of folder, wrap 8" length around folder; secure with tape. Tie 11" length into a bow. Hot glue bow to ribbon at overlap and flower to knot of bow.

easy!

MARDI GRAS MIX

*O*h me-o, my-o! Enjoy the down-South flavor of the bayou with our zesty Jambalaya Mix, presented with easy cooking directions. The recipe makes enough spicy starter to share with four families, so spreading the Fat Tuesday taste is a cinch! Make fitting packages by painting wooden boxes with glowing hues and topping them off with colorful Mardi Gras beads.

JAMBALAYA MIX

- 1/2 cup sweet pepper flakes
- 1/4 cup dried minced onions
- 1/4 cup parsley flakes
- 1/4 cup beef bouillon granules
- 3 tablespoons dried minced garlic
- 1 to 2 tablespoons ground black pepper
- 2 tablespoons paprika
- 1 tablespoon dried oregano leaves
- 2 teaspoons salt
- 1 to 2 teaspoons crushed red pepper flakes
- 1/4 to 1/2 teaspoon ground red pepper
- 1/2 teaspoon ground cumin
- 4 cups uncooked white rice, divided
- 4 bay leaves, divided

In a medium bowl, combine pepper flakes, onions, parsley, bouillon granules, garlic, black pepper, paprika, oregano, salt, red pepper flakes, red pepper, and cumin. Place 1 cup rice and 1 bay leaf in each of 4 resealable plastic bags. Divide spice mixture evenly into bags. Seal bags and give each bag with recipe for Jambalaya.

Yield: about 1 1/2 cups mix

JAMBALAYA

- 3 cups water
- 16 ounces smoked sausage, sliced
- 1 can (14 1/2 ounces) diced tomatoes, undrained
- 1 bag Jambalaya Mix

In a Dutch oven, bring water, sausage, tomatoes, and Jambalaya Mix to a boil over medium heat, stirring occasionally. Reduce heat to low. Stirring occasionally, cover and simmer 23 to 28 minutes or until most of liquid is absorbed and rice is tender. Remove bay leaf to serve. Serve warm.

Yield: about 7 cups jambalaya

MARDI GRAS BOX

You will need an oval Shaker box (we used a 4 1/2" x 6" oval box); black spray paint; gold, purple, and green acrylic paint; paintbrushes; Liquitex Painters Pearl Medium™; gold fine-point paint pen; clear spray sealer; hot glue gun; one strand each of gold, purple, and green beads; hole punch; 1 1/2" x 2 5/8" piece of black card stock; and 6" of gold cord.

Allow paint, pearl medium, paint pen, and sealer to dry after each application.

1. Remove lid from box. Spray paint box and lid black. Paint 3/4" wide gold stripes and 1" wide green and purple stripes around sides of box. Mix one part water with one part pearl medium; apply mixture over stripes. Use paint pen to write "Mardi Gras" on side of lid. Apply two to three coats of sealer to box and lid. Replace lid.
2. Arrange beads on top of lid; spot glue to secure.
3. For tag, punch hole in card stock. Use paint pen to write message on tag. Use cord to attach tag to beads.

ST. PADDY'S PIE

Share the luck o' the Irish in truly tasty style! Friends and leprechauns alike will dance with delight when they taste our French Vanilla Custard Pie. Use shamrock-motif napkins to cover a pie box; then tuck the dessert inside. Wired ribbon adds flair, and a handmade tag sends wishes for a happy St. Patrick's Day.

FRENCH VANILLA CUSTARD PIE

CRUST

- 1¹/₂ cups all-purpose flour
- 1 teaspoon grated whole nutmeg
- ¹/₂ teaspoon salt
- ¹/₂ cup vegetable shortening
- ¹/₄ cup cold water

FILLING

- 1 cup sugar
- 2 tablespoons butter or margarine, softened
- 6 eggs
- 2 cups French vanilla non-dairy liquid coffee creamer (found in dairy section)
- 1 teaspoon vanilla extract
- ¹/₂ teaspoon grated whole nutmeg
- ¹/₄ teaspoon salt

For crust, combine flour, nutmeg, and salt in a medium bowl. Using a pastry blender or 2 knives, cut in shortening until mixture resembles coarse meal. Sprinkle with water; mix until a soft dough forms. On a lightly floured surface, use a floured rolling pin to roll out dough to ¹/₈-inch thickness. Transfer to a 9-inch pie plate; use a sharp knife to trim edge of dough. Flute edge of dough.

Preheat oven to 450 degrees. For filling, beat sugar and butter in a medium bowl until well blended. Add eggs, 1 at a time, beating well after each addition. Beat in creamer, vanilla, nutmeg, and salt. Pour filling into crust. Bake 7 minutes. Reduce heat to 350 degrees and bake 25 to 30 minutes or until center is almost set. Cool pie on a wire rack 1 hour. Serve warm or chilled. Store in an airtight container in refrigerator.

Yield: about 8 servings

ST. PATRICK'S DAY PIE BOX

You will need shamrock-motif paper napkins, 9" x 9" x 4¹/₂" pie box, spray adhesive, craft knife, cutting mat, 2¹/₂ yds. of 2"w wired ribbon, white card stock, green and black permanent fine-point markers, hole punch, and ¹/₁₆"w satin ribbon.

1. Unfold and press napkins. Separate napkins into layers. Unfold box; place right side up on a flat surface. Apply spray adhesive to right side of box. Using printed layers of napkins only and overlapping as necessary, smooth napkins on box until entire box is covered. Smooth napkin edges onto wrong side of box. If box has slits, use craft knife to cut through slits from inside of box. Reassemble box. Place gift in box.

2. Beginning with center of wired ribbon across top of box, wrap ribbon to bottom, twist ribbon, and bring ends to top of box; tie into a bow.

3. For tag, cut a 2" x 3" piece from card stock. Cut desired motif from napkin. Apply spray adhesive to wrong side of motif; smooth onto one corner of card stock. Trimming around edge of motif, trim ¹/₄" from long edge (top) of tag. Use green marker to draw "stitches" along edges and black marker to write message on tag. Punch hole in tag. Use satin ribbon to attach tag to bow.

EASTER BASKET

*T*he Easter Bunny's on his way, and he's toting a basket of elegant goodies! To make these easy-to-decorate treats, simply dip chocolate sandwich cookies into candy coating and drizzle them with pastel stripes. A gingham bow and handmade tag add a perky touch to the picket fence basket.

WHITE CHOCOLATE EASTER COOKIES

For a smooth coating, use a pastry brush to remove loose crumbs from cookies.

20 ounces white candy coating, divided
6 ounces white baking chocolate, chopped
1 package (16 ounces) chocolate sandwich cookies
Pink, green, blue, and yellow paste food coloring

Chop 18 ounces candy coating. In top of a double boiler, melt chopped candy coating and chocolate over hot, not simmering, water. Dip each cookie into chocolate. Place on a baking sheet lined with lightly greased waxed paper. Add remaining 2 ounces candy coating to double boiler and melt. Place 1 tablespoon candy coating in a small bowl; tint light pink. Spoon into a small plastic bag. Snip off 1 corner of bag to create a small opening. Drizzle coating over cookies. Repeat with remaining food coloring. Let coating harden. Store in an airtight container in a cool place.

Yield: about 3¹/₂ dozen cookies

PICKET FENCE BASKET

You will need a paintbrush, pink acrylic paint, 7¹/₂" x 9" white wooden picket fence basket with handle, hot glue gun, 4"h Easter-motif ornament, shredded paper, 2 yds. of ⁷/₈"w ribbon, 6" of floral wire, pink and green colored pencils, photocopy of tag design (page 149) on white card stock, craft glue stick, pink card stock, and decorative-edge craft scissors.

1. Use end of paintbrush to paint pink dots on handle of basket; allow to dry. Hot glue ornament to handle. Fill basket with shredded paper.

2. Knot a 6" length of ribbon around basket handle. Use remaining ribbon and follow *Making a Bow*, page 153, to make a bow with eight 6" loops and two 8" streamers. Use wire to attach bow to knot of ribbon on handle.

3. Use colored pencils to color tag; cut out. Use glue stick to glue tag to pink card stock. Leaving a ¹/₂" pink border, use craft scissors to cut out tag. Use colored pencils to outline tag and draw border along edges. Hot glue tag to center front of basket.

"EGG-CELLENT" SURPRISES

*D*ecoupaged with colorful
bits of tissue paper, tiny oval boxes
make "egg-cellent" containers for
hiding our Chocolate-Covered Jelly
Beans. Top them with sheer bows
for sweet Easter surprises!

CHOCOLATE-COVERED JELLY BEANS

- 6 ounces chocolate candy coating, chopped
- 8 ounces small red gourmet jelly beans (we used cherry)
- 8 ounces small pink, purple, and white gourmet jelly beans

In a small saucepan, melt candy
coating over low heat. Remove from heat
(if coating begins to harden, return to
heat). Place ¹/₂ cup red jelly beans in
coating. Using a fork, remove a few jelly
beans at a time; shake off excess coating.
Place on baking sheet lined with waxed
paper. Repeat with remaining red jelly
beans. Let chocolate harden. Combine
chocolate-covered jelly beans with
remaining jelly beans. Store in an airtight
container in a cool place.

Yield: about 3 cups candies

DECOUPAGED EGG BOXES

For each box, you will need pink, purple,
and blue tissue paper; decoupage glue;
paintbrush; 3¹/₂" x 4¹/₂" oval papier-
mâché box with lid; clear varnish; one
14" length and one 30" length of ³/₄"w
sheer ribbon; and 6" of floral wire.

1. Tear tissue paper into small pieces.
Refer to *Decoupage*, page 152, to apply
tissue pieces to box and lid; allow to dry.
Allowing to dry between applications,

apply two to three coats of varnish to box
and lid.
2. Place gift in box.
3. Knot 14" ribbon length around box.
Use remaining ribbon length and follow

Making a Bow, page 153, to make a bow
with four 4" loops, two 3" loops, 1"
center loop, and two 3" streamers. Use
wire to attach bow to knot of ribbon.

115

REFRESHING RELISH

*I*t's a little bit tart and a little bit tangy — and absolutely delicious! This refreshing Cherry-Onion Relish is delightful served with meats. Paint simple flower designs on a petite canvas bag to deliver the condiment in springtime style.

CHERRY-ONION RELISH

2 jars (12 ounces each) cherry preserves
1 cup finely chopped red onion
¼ cup sugar
2 tablespoons apple cider vinegar
1 tablespoon finely chopped crystallized ginger

In a medium saucepan, combine preserves, onion, sugar, vinegar, and ginger. Stirring frequently, bring to a boil over medium heat. Continuing to stir, cook 15 minutes or until onion is tender and mixture thickens. Serve warm or at room temperature. Store in an airtight container in refrigerator.

Yield: about 2½ cups relish

PAINTED FLOWER BAG

You will need tracing paper; transfer paper; 4¼" x 5¾" canvas bag; yellow, pink, and blue acrylic paint; paintbrushes; black permanent fine-point marker; 12" lengths of assorted ribbons; fabric glue; and six assorted buttons.

Allow paint and glue to dry after each application.

1. Trace design, page 145, onto tracing paper. Use transfer paper to transfer design to front of bag.

2. Paint flowers. Use marker to draw over stems and outline flowers.

3. Tie ribbon lengths together into a bow. Glue buttons to flowers and to top of each stem. Glue bow to stems.

HATS OFF TO MOTHERS

*H*ats off to loving mothers everywhere! This Peppermint Candy Fudge is almost as sweet as dear ol' Mom. Flavored with crushed peppermint candies, each tidbit is simply delicious. Paint a hat-shaped box in pastel colors and tie on a fancy beribboned flower for Mother's Day.

PEPPERMINT CANDY FUDGE

Candies can be ground in a coffee mill or crushed with a hammer.

FUDGE
- 2 cups sugar
- 1 cup finely ground peppermint candies (about 42 round candies), divided
- 1 cup evaporated milk
- ¹/₂ cup butter or margarine
- ¹/₂ teaspoon salt
- 1 package (12 ounces) semisweet chocolate chips
- 1 jar (7 ounces) marshmallow creme
- ¹/₂ teaspoon vanilla extract

GLAZE
- ³/₄ cup confectioners sugar
- 4 teaspoons milk

For fudge, line an 8-inch square baking pan with aluminum foil, extending foil over 2 sides of pan; grease foil. In a heavy large saucepan, combine sugar, ³/₄ cup candies, evaporated milk, butter, and salt. Stirring constantly, bring to a boil over medium heat. Continuing to stir, boil 5 minutes. Remove from heat and stir in chocolate chips, marshmallow creme, and vanilla; stir until smooth. Pour into prepared pan. Chill 2 hours or until firm. Use ends of foil to lift candy from pan.

Cut into 1-inch squares. Place pieces of fudge on a wire rack with waxed paper underneath.

For glaze, combine confectioners sugar, remaining ¹/₄ cup candies, and milk in a small bowl; stir until smooth. Spoon glaze into a resealable plastic bag. Snip off 1 corner of bag to create a small opening; drizzle glaze over fudge. Let glaze harden. Store in a single layer in an airtight container in refrigerator.

Yield: about 4 dozen pieces fudge

PAINTED HAT BOX

You will need a hat-shaped papier-mâché box (we used a box with a 12" dia. brim and 8¹/₄" dia. crown), white spray paint, yellow and pink acrylic paint, household sponge, flat and liner paintbrushes,

1¹/₃ yds. of 2¹/₄"w sheer floral ribbon, hot glue gun, and a 4" dia. artificial flower.

Allow paint to dry after each application.

1. Remove lid from box. Spray paint lid and box white. Follow *Sponge Painting*, page 153, to paint sides of lid yellow. To paint yellow lines, dip tips of flat paintbrush bristles in water, then dab corner of bristles in yellow paint. Stroke brush on palette until there is a gradual change from paint to water. Paint yellow lines on top of lid. Use liner paintbrush to paint pink lines along edges of yellow lines. Paint pink "squiggles" on top of lid and brim of box.
2. Place gift in box; replace lid. Tie ribbon into a bow around lid. Glue flower to knot of bow.

COMING UP ROSES

Honor Mom on her special day with this Rosy Angel Food Cake. Rose-flavored icing spills over a delicate cake for a beautiful treat! Top the gorgeous dessert with a lacy nosegay of silk roses; then present it with a touching handmade card.

ROSY ANGEL FOOD CAKE

Depending on the brand, rose water varies in flavor intensity.

    1 package (16 ounces) angel food
       cake mix
    3 to 4 teaspoons rose water, divided
       (available at gourmet food
       stores)
       Pink paste food coloring
    1½ cups confectioners sugar
    1½ to 2 tablespoons water

Preheat oven to 350 degrees. Prepare cake mix according to package directions, stirring in 2 to 3 teaspoons rose water; tint batter pink. Pour into an ungreased 10-inch tube pan. Bake 43 to 48 minutes or until top is golden brown. Invert pan; cool cake completely.

Transfer cake to a serving plate. Combine confectioners sugar, water, and ½ to 1 teaspoon rose water in a small bowl; tint pink. Drizzle glaze over cake. Store in an airtight container.

Yield: about 12 servings

HANDMADE PAPER CARD

You will need a 9" x 12" piece of pink card stock, decorative-edge craft scissors, handmade paper, vellum, spray adhesive, craft glue, silk flower petals and leaves, colored pencils, ⅛" dia. hole punch, 6" of ⅝"w wired gold ribbon, and a gold fine-point paint pen.

Use craft glue for all gluing unless otherwise indicated. Allow glue to dry after each application.

1. For card, match short edges and fold card stock in half. Use craft scissors to cut a 4½" x 7½" piece each from handmade paper and vellum. Apply spray adhesive to wrong side of handmade paper; center and smooth onto front of card.
2. Arrange and glue flower petals and leaves on handmade paper. Use colored pencils to draw additional greenery and stems.
3. Glue edges of vellum to edges of handmade paper. Punch two holes ¾" apart at top center of card front. Insert ribbon ends from outside to inside of card. Crossing ends inside card, thread ends through opposite holes to outside of card. Pull ribbon ends taut; notch ends.
4. Use paint pen to draw design along edges and write "Happy Mother's Day" on front of card.

TUSSIE-MUSSIE

You will need a 6" dia. white paper doily, two artificial miniature rosebuds with leaves, small flower sprigs, craft wire, and wire cutters.

1. Fold doily in half from top to bottom, then again from left to right. Trim ⅜" from pointed tip of doily.
2. Inserting stems through hole in doily, arrange rosebuds and flower sprigs in doily. Gather doily around stems; use wire to secure stems and doily.
3. Place tussie-mussie at center top of cake.

DAD'S DAY SNACK SACK

Whether he's on the go or relaxing in front of the TV, Dad will savor every morsel of this super snack mix. It's jammed full of his favorite munchies, including popcorn, nuts, and corn chips! He'll appreciate the big decorated bag, and our recipe makes enough that he won't have to hunt for more.

SAVORY SNACK MIX

- 12 cups popped popcorn
- 6 cups corn chips
- 1 package (10 ounces) cheese snack crackers
- 3 cups pecan halves
- 1 cup butter or margarine
- 1/4 cup Worcestershire sauce
- 1 tablespoon ground cumin
- 2 teaspoons garlic salt
- 1/2 teaspoon ground red pepper

Preheat oven to 250 degrees. Combine popcorn, corn chips, crackers, and pecans in a large roasting pan. In a small saucepan, melt butter over medium-low heat. Remove from heat and stir in Worcestershire sauce, cumin, garlic salt, and red pepper. Pour over popcorn mixture; stir until well coated. Bake 1 hour, stirring every 15 minutes. Spread on aluminum foil to cool. Store in an airtight container.

Yield: about 19 cups snack mix

FATHER'S DAY BAG

You will need a heavyweight brown paper bag (we used an 8" x 17½" bag); yardstick; brown and black permanent fine-point markers; masculine-motif wallpaper border; spray adhesive; hot

glue gun; ³/₈" dia. rope; hole punch; several 20" lengths each of natural, green, and black raffia; miniature pinecone pick; 4" x 5" piece of corrugated craft cardboard; 2½" x 3" piece of kraft paper; garden clippers; several small twigs; and a jumbo paper clip.

1. Carefully open bag at seams; lay bag flat. Use yardstick and brown marker to draw vertical stripes ³/₄" apart on bag.
2. Measure width of bag. Cut a piece from wallpaper the determined measurement. Apply spray adhesive to wrong side of wallpaper; smooth onto bag. Reassemble bag; hot glue seams to secure.
3. Cut two lengths from rope the determined width measurement. Hot

glue to front of bag along top and bottom edges of wallpaper.
4. Punch two holes through front and back of bag 1" apart at center top of bag. Place gift in bag. Thread raffia through holes and tie into a bow at front of bag. Apply hot glue to end of pinecone pick; insert under knot of bow.
5. For tag, cut a 3" x 4" piece from wallpaper. Center and hot glue wallpaper piece on cardboard. Center and hot glue kraft paper on wallpaper piece. Using garden clippers and trimming to fit, hot glue twigs along top, bottom, then side edges of kraft paper. Cut one motif from wallpaper; hot glue to tag. Use black marker to write message on tag. Use paper clip to attach tag to bag.

THANKS, DAD!

*D*ads deserve thanks for all the special things they do, so express your gratitude in a tasty way! Our Chocolate Gingersnaps are irresistible, and they're even better accompanied by a cup of freshly brewed coffee. Trim a hand-painted terra-cotta pot with coffee beans and include a bag of his favorite coffee for a Father's Day treat!

CHOCOLATE GINGERSNAPS

- 1¹/₂ cups butter or margarine, softened
- 2³/₄ cups sugar, divided
- 2 eggs
- ¹/₂ cup molasses
- 4 cups all-purpose flour
- ¹/₄ cup plus 2 tablespoons cocoa, divided
- 2 teaspoons baking soda
- 2 teaspoons ground cinnamon
- 2 teaspoons ground cloves
- 2 teaspoons ground ginger

Preheat oven to 375 degrees. In a large bowl, cream butter and 2 cups sugar until fluffy. Add eggs and molasses; beat until smooth. In a medium bowl, combine flour, ¹/₄ cup cocoa, baking soda, cinnamon, cloves, and ginger. Add dry ingredients to creamed mixture; stir until a soft dough forms. In a small bowl, combine remaining ³/₄ cup sugar and 2 tablespoons cocoa. Shape dough into 1-inch balls; roll in sugar mixture. Place balls 3 inches apart on a lightly greased baking sheet. Flatten balls into 2-inch-diameter cookies with bottom of a glass dipped in sugar mixture. Bake 5 to 7 minutes or until bottoms are lightly browned. Transfer cookies to a wire rack to cool. Store in an airtight container.

Yield: about 10 dozen cookies

COFFEE-BEAN POT

You will need ecru, brown, and black acrylic paint; paintbrushes; 6" dia. terra-cotta flowerpot; tracing paper; transfer paper; hot glue gun; coffee beans; clear gloss varnish; craft glue stick; 2¹/₂" x 3¹/₂" piece of ecru card stock; 3" x 4" piece of brown card stock; and a black permanent fine-point marker.

Allow paint and varnish to dry after each application.

1. Paint outside of flowerpot below rim ecru. Paint inside of flowerpot and outside of rim brown. Beginning with stripes 1" wide below rim and tapering slightly at bottom, paint brown stripes evenly around flowerpot.

2. Trace pattern, page 145, onto tracing paper. Using transfer paper, transfer three coffee cup designs around flowerpot. Paint coffee cup designs black.

3. Hot glue coffee beans around outside rim of flowerpot.

4. Apply two coats of varnish to inside and outside of flowerpot.

5. For tag, use glue stick to glue ecru card stock to brown card stock. Use marker to draw border and write message on tag.

RED, WHITE, & BLUE TRIBUTE

*H*ave a sweet Fourth of July with a taste-tempting dessert pizza. Folks will rave over the creamy treat, which is swirled with cherry and blueberry preserves. Pay tribute to the red, white, and blue holiday by packing the treat in a paper-covered take-out box topped with button stars.

CHERRY-BLUEBERRY PIZZA

CRUST
- 3/4 cup slivered almonds, toasted
- 1 1/4 cups all-purpose flour
- 1/2 cup sugar
- 3/4 cup butter, softened
- 1 egg

FILLING
- 4 ounces cream cheese, softened
- 1/4 cup sugar
- 1 tablespoon all-purpose flour
- 1 teaspoon vanilla extract
- 1/4 cup cherry preserves
- 1/4 cup blueberry preserves

Preheat oven to 350 degrees. For crust, process almonds in a food processor until coarsely ground. Add flour and sugar; pulse process until blended. Add butter and egg; process until a soft dough forms. Spread mixture into a greased 12-inch-diameter pizza pan. Bake 25 minutes or until crust begins to brown.

For filling, beat cream cheese and sugar in a small bowl until fluffy. Beat in flour and vanilla until blended. Spread mixture over crust. Drop teaspoonfuls of preserves over cream cheese mixture. Using tip of a knife, lightly swirl preserves. Bake 20 to 24 minutes in a 350-degree

oven or until cream cheese mixture is lightly browned. Cool in pan on a wire rack. Cut into wedges. Store in an airtight container in refrigerator. Serve chilled or at room temperature.

Yield: about 1 dozen pieces

PATRIOTIC PIZZA BOX

You will need a 14 1/2" square pizza box, red stripe wrapping paper, spray adhesive, craft knife, cutting mat, hot glue gun, 30 white buttons, 7" x 8" piece of blue card stock, white fine-point paint pen, and a craft glue stick.

1. Unfold box. Cut a piece from wrapping paper 1" larger on all sides than unfolded box. Place wrapping paper right side down on a flat surface.
2. Apply spray adhesive to outside of box. Center box adhesive side down on paper; press firmly to secure.
3. Use craft knife to cut paper even with edges of box. If box has slits, use craft knife to cut through slits from inside of box. Reassemble box.
4. Arrange and hot glue buttons on card stock. Use paint pen to draw "stitches" along edges of card stock. Use glue stick to glue card stock on box.

ALL-AMERICAN POPCORN

Let's hear it for Uncle Sam! Our fruity candied popcorn is a fitting snack for a patriotic occasion. Create an explosive summer treat by transforming an ordinary tin into a colorful hat!

ALL-AMERICAN POPCORN

Make separate recipes of red and blue popcorn; mix with 20 cups of plain popcorn.

- 20 cups popped popcorn
- 2 cups sugar
- ¹/₂ cup butter or margarine
- ¹/₂ cup light corn syrup
- ¹/₄ teaspoon salt
- 1 package (3 ounces) cherry *or* blueberry gelatin
- Red *or* blue paste food coloring

Preheat oven to 275 degrees. Place popcorn in a large greased roasting pan. In a large heavy saucepan, combine sugar, butter, corn syrup, and salt. Stirring constantly, bring to a boil over medium heat; boil 5 minutes. Remove from heat. For red popcorn, stir in cherry gelatin and red food coloring; for blue popcorn, stir in blueberry gelatin and blue food coloring. Pour sugar mixture over popcorn, stirring to coat. Bake 30 minutes, stirring every 10 minutes. Spread on ungreased aluminum foil to cool. Store in an airtight container.

Yield: about 22 cups flavored popcorn

UNCLE SAM'S HAT

You will need a 10" dia. tin with lid, corrugated cardboard, white and blue spray paint, ⁷/₈"w red grosgrain ribbon, spray adhesive, hot glue gun, tracing

paper, compressed craft sponge, paper towels, white acrylic paint, and a red fine-point paint pen.

Allow paint and paint pen to dry after each application.

1. Draw around tin on cardboard. Cut out circle 2" outside drawn line. Spray paint cardboard blue. Spray paint outside of tin and lid white.

2. Place lid on tin. Measure height between rim of lid and bottom rim of tin.

Cut 18 strips of ribbon the determined measurement. Apply spray adhesive to wrong side of ribbon strips; smooth strips ⁷/₈" apart around tin. Center and hot glue tin on cardboard.

3. Trace pattern, page 133, onto tracing paper; cut out. Draw around pattern on sponge; cut out. Follow *Sponge Painting,* page 153, to paint white stars around cardboard.

4. Use pen to write message on top of lid.

BOO JUICE

*N*o Halloween party would be complete without peppy "Pumpkin" Boo Juice! This yummy thirst-quencher, packed with orange, carrot, strawberry, and banana flavors, looks like it's freshly squeezed from a pumpkin. Tote the drink in a painted bottle topped with a fabric circle and a mesh ribbon bow. Include a "creepy" tag to announce your present.

"PUMPKIN" BOO JUICE

- 1 bottle (64 ounces) carrot, strawberry, and banana drink
- 1 can (14 ounces) sweetened condensed milk
- 1 cup water
- 1/2 cup sugar
- 1 package (0.15 ounce) unsweetened orange-flavored soft drink mix

In a 1-gallon container, combine drink, sweetened condensed milk, water, sugar, and drink mix; stir until well blended. Cover and store in refrigerator. Serve chilled.

Yield: about 12 cups drink

SPOOKY SPIDER BOTTLE

You will need clear self-adhesive plastic, clean 2-liter plastic bottle with cap (label removed), black spray primer, black spray paint, black enamel paint, liner paintbrush, 1 yd. of 3¹/2"w orange-and-black mesh wired ribbon, 8" of craft wire, 6" circle of fabric, and photocopy of tag design (page 146) on orange card stock.

Allow primer and paint to dry after each application.

1. Trace spiderweb pattern, page 146, onto paper side of plastic; cut out shape. Remove paper from plastic; apply shape to bottle.
2. Apply primer to bottle. Spray paint bottle black. Remove shape from bottle; discard.
3. Use enamel paint to paint spiderweb lines on unpainted part of bottle.

4. Use ribbon and follow *Making a Bow*, page 153, to make a bow with four 6" loops, a center loop, and two 4" streamers.
5. Fill bottle with juice. Place cap on bottle. For cap cover, center fabric circle over cap. Use wire to attach bow and secure cap cover.
6. Cut out tag.

DELICIOUSLY SPOOKY

*T*his appetizer is so
delicious, it's spooky! Russian-
style salad dressing adds zip to
a creamy blend of cheeses, and
chopped black olives are perfect
for adding the jack-o'-lantern
face. Present the cheese spread
and some crackers on a fabric-
covered wooden tray.

JACK-O'-LANTERN CHEESE SPREAD

    4 cups (16 ounces) shredded sharp
         Cheddar cheese
    1 package (8 ounces) cream cheese,
         softened
  1/2 cup Russian-style salad dressing
    3 tablespoons chopped black olives
       Crackers to serve

Line an 8-inch round cake pan with
plastic wrap; lightly oil plastic wrap.
Process cheeses and salad dressing in a
food processor until well blended. Spread
cheese mixture into prepared pan. Cover
and chill 2 hours or until firm.

Use ends of plastic wrap to remove
cheese from pan. Invert cheese onto
serving plate. Smooth top and sides of
cheese with a small metal spatula. Use a
toothpick to draw outline of eyes, nose,
and mouth of jack-o'-lantern on cheese
mixture. Fill in outlines with olives. Serve
at room temperature with crackers. Store
in an airtight container in refrigerator.

Yield: about 3½ cups cheese spread

HALLOWEEN TRAY

You will need clear self-adhesive plastic,
Halloween-motif fabric for liner, 15" dia.
wooden serving tray, and spray adhesive.

1. Apply plastic to right side of fabric.
2. Draw around tray on wrong side of
fabric. Cut out circle just inside drawn
line. Place circle in bottom of tray.
3. Measure around tray; add 1/2".
Measure height of side of tray. Cut a
strip from fabric the determined
measurements. Apply spray adhesive to
wrong side of fabric; smooth around side
of tray.

PUMPKIN PATCH CRUNCH

Who needs to put on a costume and go door-to-door when the best treat can be found in these colorful appliquéd tins! Our Cashew Popcorn Crunch is a tasty snack no goblin can resist!

CASHEW POPCORN CRUNCH

- 16 cups popped popcorn
- 2 cans (10 ounces each) cashews
- 2 cups firmly packed brown sugar
- 1/2 cup butter or margarine
- 1/2 cup light corn syrup
- 1/4 teaspoon salt
- 1/4 teaspoon amaretto-flavored oil (used in candy making)
- 1/2 teaspoon baking soda

Preheat oven to 275 degrees. Combine popcorn and cashews in a large roasting pan. In a heavy large saucepan, combine brown sugar, butter, corn syrup, and salt. Stirring constantly, bring to a boil over medium heat. Boil 5 minutes without stirring. Remove from heat; stir in flavored oil and baking soda (mixture will foam). Pour syrup over popcorn mixture; stir until well coated. Bake 45 minutes, stirring every 10 minutes. Spread on aluminum foil to cool. Store in an airtight container.

Yield: about 21 cups popcorn

APPLIQUÉD PUMPKIN TINS

For each tin, you will need a tin (we used a 4" square and a 7" round tin), black spray primer, black spray paint, assorted fabrics, spray adhesive, craft glue, rickrack and jumbo rickrack to coordinate with fabrics, paper-backed fusible web, pressing cloth, poster board, decorative-edge craft scissors, photocopy of tag design (page 139) on purple card stock, and a black permanent fine-point marker.

Use craft glue for all gluing unless otherwise indicated. Allow glue to dry after each application.

1. Remove lid from tin. Apply primer to tin; allow to dry. Spray paint tin black; allow to dry.
2. Draw around lid on wrong side of fabric. Cut out fabric 2" outside drawn line. Apply spray adhesive to wrong side of fabric. Overlapping excess fabric to inside of lid, center and smooth fabric on lid. Spot glue as necessary.

3. Trimming to fit, glue jumbo rickrack, then rickrack around lid and/or tin.
4. Use patterns, page 148, and follow *Making Appliqués,* page 152, to make desired number of pumpkin and stem appliqués from fabrics. Arrange appliqués on tin. Using pressing cloth, fuse appliqués in place.
5. Cut a 2 1/2" x 3 1/2" piece each from poster board, fabric, and fusible web; fuse fabric to poster board. Use craft scissors to trim edges of fabric-covered poster board. Use marker to write message on tag. Cut out tag. Glue tag to fabric-covered poster board; allow to dry.

THANKSGIVING HARVEST

*C*elebrate the harvest season by sharing bags of Hot and Sweet Tidbits. Cereal, popcorn, nuts, and candy combine to create a festive fall treat. Wrapped in paper "corn husks" and displayed in a basket, this eye-catching snack is a bounty of flavor!

HOT AND SWEET TIDBITS

- 1 package (14 ounces) honey-nut round toasted oat cereal
- 1 package (12 ounces) square corn cereal
- 8 cups popped popcorn
- 1 can (11 1/2 ounces) mixed nuts
- 1/2 cup butter or margarine
- 1/2 cup light corn syrup
- 1/2 cup small red cinnamon candies
- 1/2 cup sugar
- 1 tablespoon chili powder
- 1/4 teaspoon salt
- 1/4 teaspoon ground red pepper
- 1 package (16 ounces) candy-coated peanut butter pieces

Preheat oven to 250 degrees. In a large greased roasting pan, combine cereals, popcorn, and nuts. In a medium saucepan, combine butter, corn syrup, cinnamon candies, sugar, chili powder, salt, and red pepper. Stirring constantly, bring to a boil over medium heat. Continue stirring until candies melt. Pour over cereal mixture; stir until well coated. Bake 1 hour, stirring every 15 minutes. Spread on aluminum foil; cool completely. Add peanut butter pieces. Store in an airtight container.

Yield: about 34 cups snack mix

"CORN HUSKS" AND BASKET LINER

For each ear, you will need a 12" square of clear cellophane, transparent tape, two 22" lengths of 4"w brown paper twist, hot glue gun, two 8" lengths of jute twine, decorative-edge craft scissors, gold card stock, craft glue stick, 1 1/2" x 2 1/2" torn piece of ecru handmade paper, black permanent fine-point marker, and a 1/8" dia. hole punch.

You will also need fabric for basket liner and a basket (we used a 9 1/2" x 10 1/2" oval basket with handle).

1. Place 2 cups of tidbits (from recipe this page) at center of cellophane. Leaving 2 1/2" free at each end, roll cellophane around tidbits to form a 2" dia. by 7" long roll. Twist ends of cellophane and secure with tape.

2. For each husk, untwist paper twist pieces. Overlapping 1/2", hot glue paper twist pieces together along one long edge. Matching short edges, fold husk in half. Center wrapped tidbits on husk. Gathering at each end, shape husk around tidbits. Fold one length of twine in half; fray ends. Place folded end of twine in gathers above tidbits. Twist end of husk around twine; hot glue to secure. Twist opposite end of husk; hot glue to secure.

3. Use craft scissors to cut a 1 1/4" x 2 1/4" piece from card stock. Use glue stick to glue card stock to handmade paper. Use marker to write message on tag. Punch hole in tag. Use twine to attach tag to husk.

4. Use fabric and follow *Making a Basket Liner*, page 152, to make a liner with unfinished edges. Place liner and ears in basket.

SAVE THE TURKEYS!

Help save the Thanksgiving turkeys! Share this zesty Cranberry Meat Sauce — its zippy flavors are best served with ham or beef, so feathered friends can breathe a sigh of relief. Pack a jar of the cranberry condiment in a can dressed up in vibrant foam feathers. A wooden ball provides a head for our sign-toting tom.

CRANBERRY MEAT SAUCE

1 bottle (24 ounces) ketchup
1 can (16 ounces) whole berry cranberry sauce
1 can (16 ounces) jellied cranberry sauce
3 tablespoons prepared horseradish
2 teaspoons balsamic vinegar

In a medium saucepan, combine ketchup, cranberry sauces, horseradish, and vinegar. Stirring frequently, bring mixture to a boil over medium heat. Store in an airtight container in refrigerator. Serve as a dipping sauce or use as a glaze with meat.

Yield: about 5 cups sauce

TURKEY CAN

You will need brown acrylic paint; paintbrush; 2" dia. unfinished wooden ball with flat bottom for head; jar with lid; tracing paper; yellow, orange, red, blue, green, tan, brown, and grey craft foam; felt hat with 1$7/8$" dia. opening; craft knife; cutting mat; can large enough to accommodate jar; spray adhesive; low-temperature glue gun; two $1/4$" dia. wiggle eyes; black permanent fine-point marker; and a 3$1/2$" long craft pick.

Use low-temperature glue gun for all gluing unless otherwise indicated.

1. Paint wooden ball and jar lid brown; allow to dry.
2. Trace patterns, page 148, onto tracing paper; cut out. Draw around patterns on craft foam and cut beak from yellow foam; wattle and one feather from red foam; two wings and two feathers from tan foam; and two feathers each from orange, blue, and green foam.
3. For hatband, measure around hat crown; cut a strip from brown foam $3/8$"w by the determined measurement. For hat buckle, cut a $3/8$" x $1/2$" piece from tan foam. Use craft knife to cut a small opening at center of buckle.
4. To cover can, measure height of can; measure around can. Cut a piece from brown foam the determined measurements. Apply spray adhesive to foam. Wrap foam around can; glue seam to secure.
5. Overlapping feathers at bottom, arrange and glue feathers on back of can. Leaving 2" of pointed end of left wing unglued, glue wings on body. Glue bottom of head to center of lid, hat to head, hatband to hat, and buckle to hatband. Glue eyes, wattle, and beak to head. Place lid on jar; place jar in can.
6. For tag, cut a 2" x 3" piece from grey foam. Use marker to write message on tag. Glue one end of craft pick to center back of tag. Fold left wing over opposite end of pick; glue to secure.

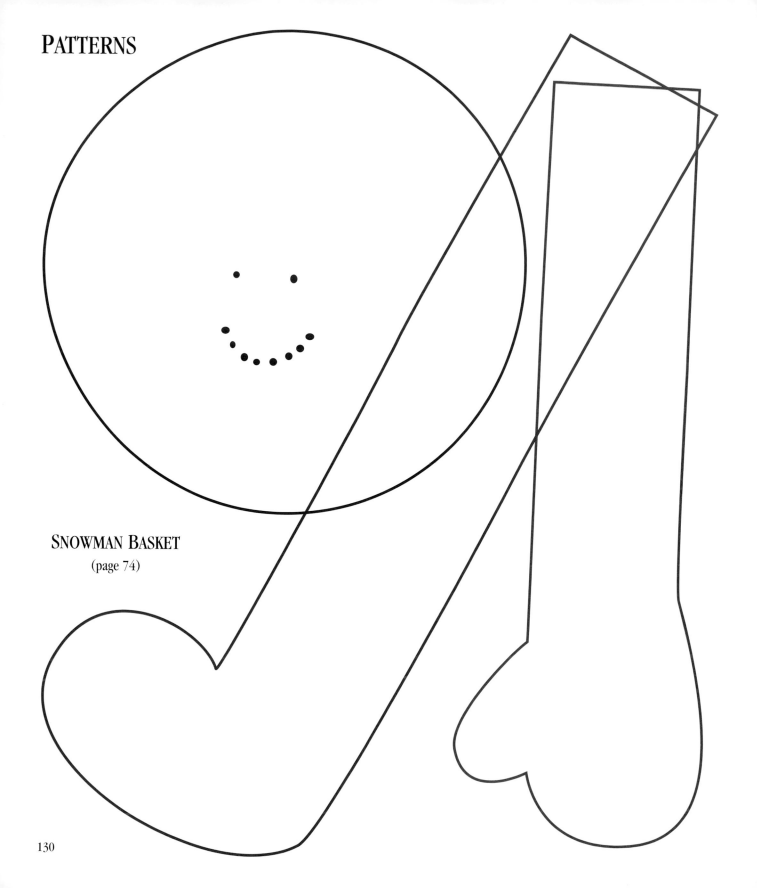

PATTERNS

SNOWMAN BASKET

(page 74)

"BELIEVE" CROSS-STITCHED TOWEL (page 53)

X	DMC	¼ X	BS'T	ANC.	COLOR
•	blanc		✚	2	white
■	310		✚	403	black
▣	321			9046	red
▥	415			398	dk grey
▤	666			46	lt red
✳	676			891	gold
◈	677	◹		886	lt gold
◉	761			1021	salmon
╱	762	◹		234	grey
▦	792	◺		941	vy dk blue
◨	793	◺		176	dk blue
V	794	◹		175	blue
▩	840			379	brown
■	910			229	green
◈	911			205	lt green
	938		╱	381	dk brown
4	948	◹		1011	flesh
△	3799			236	charcoal grey
•	938			381	dk brown
					Fr. Knot

STAR BASKET LINER
(page 43)

ELF BAG
(page 31)

PATTERNS (continued)

CUTOUT TREE BAGS
(page 64)

MOOSE BAG
(page 57)

SNOW LADY BAG
(page 38)

UNCLE SAM'S HAT
(page 123)

MOOSE BAG
(page 57)

PATTERNS (continued)

"PENNY RUG" BASKET
(page 59)

SANTA-FACE TOWEL BAGS
(page 15)

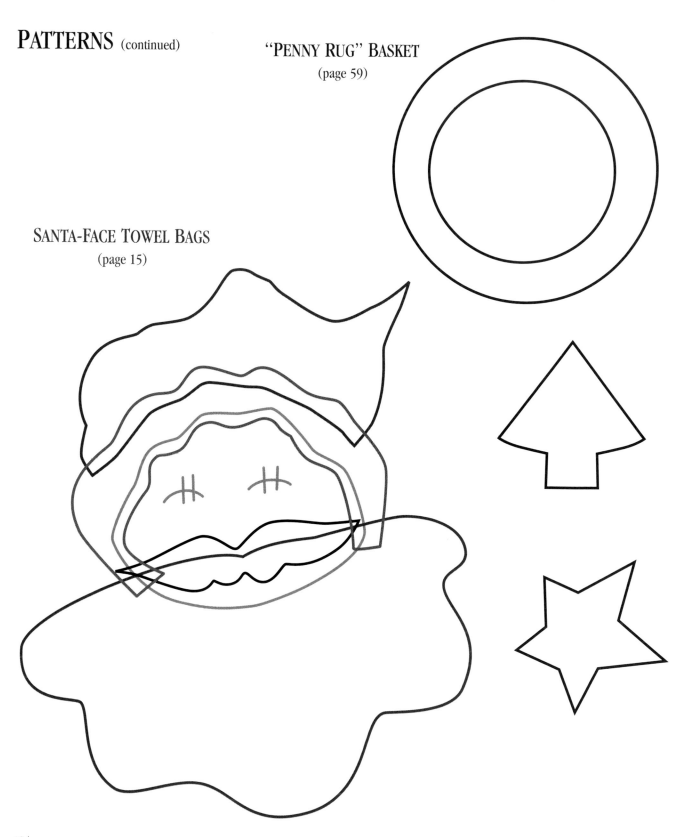

MITTEN BOX
(page 29)

SANTA JAR
(page 56)

PAINTED COASTERS AND BAG
(page 37)

135

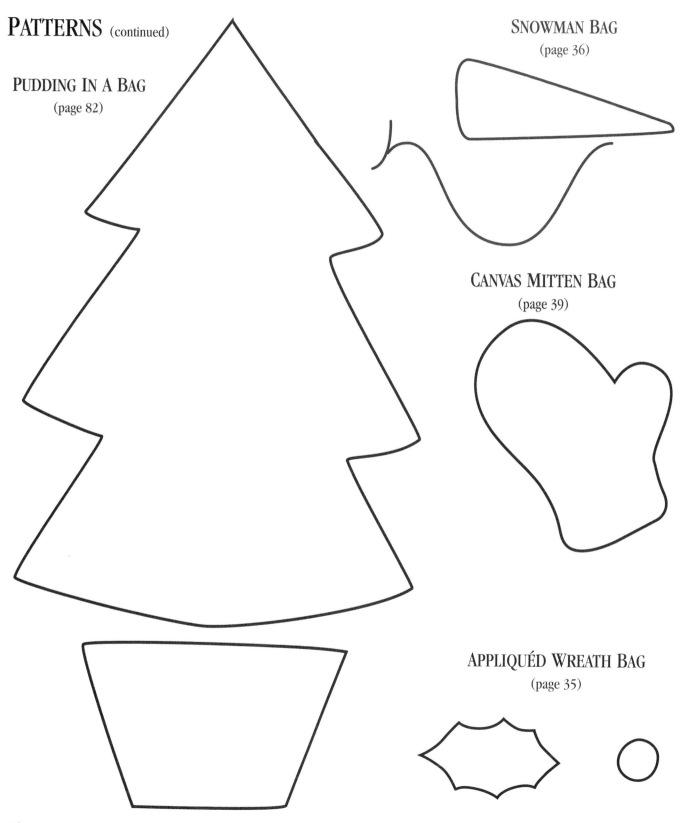

PATTERNS (continued)

PUDDING IN A BAG
(page 82)

SNOWMAN BAG
(page 36)

CANVAS MITTEN BAG
(page 39)

APPLIQUÉD WREATH BAG
(page 35)

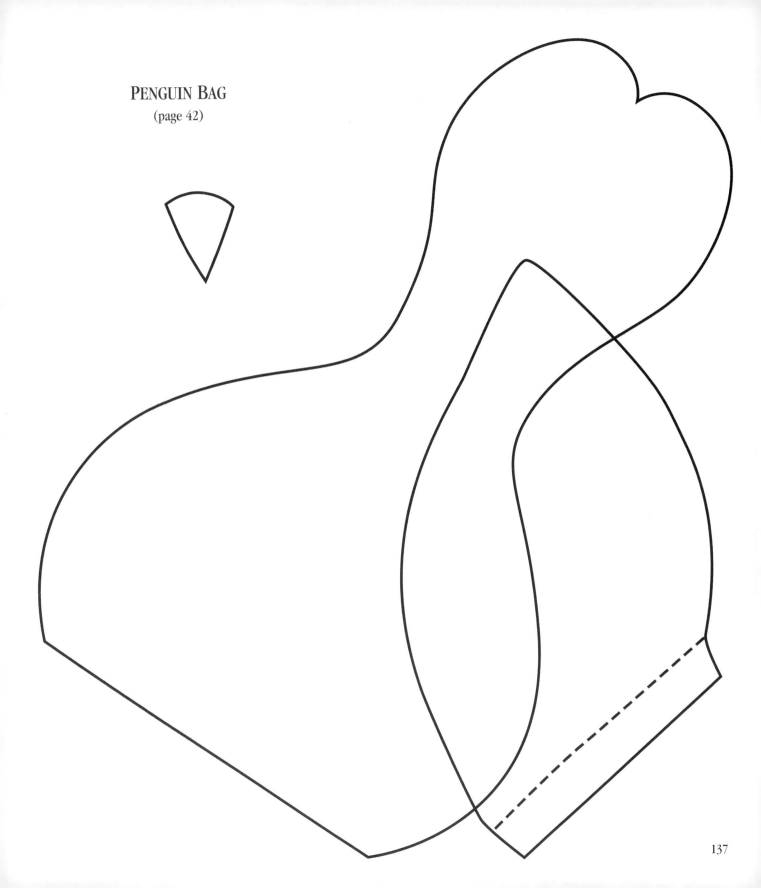

PENGUIN BAG
(page 42)

PATTERNS (continued)

GINGERBREAD BASKET AND APRON
(page 32)

"I LOVE CHOCOLATE" BASKET
(page 100)

I ♡ Chocolate

PEPPERMINT BOXES
(page 14)

APPLIQUÉD PUMPKIN TINS
(page 126)

ELFIN SANTA BAG
(page 18)

TIMBERMAN'S BASKET
(page 66)

ANGEL ORNAMENT BASKET
(page 16)

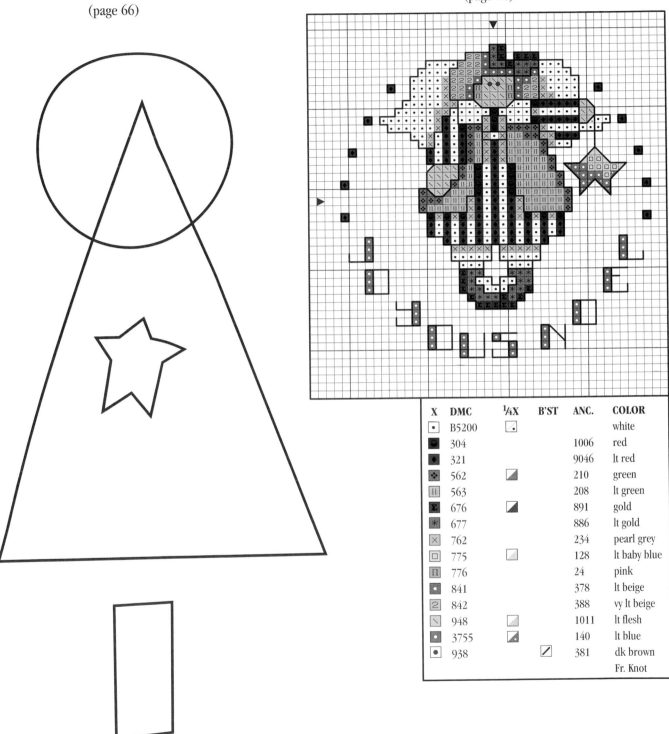

X	DMC	¼X	B'ST	ANC.	COLOR
•	B5200	•			white
	304			1006	red
	321			9046	lt red
	562	/		210	green
‖	563			208	lt green
	676	/		891	gold
*	677			886	lt gold
×	762			234	pearl grey
□	775	/		128	lt baby blue
⊓	776			24	pink
	841			378	lt beige
2	842			388	vy lt beige
＼	948	/		1011	lt flesh
	3755	/		140	lt blue
•	938		/	381	dk brown
					Fr. Knot

PATTERNS (continued)

COOKIE BASKET (page 68)

X	DMC	¼X	B'ST	ANC.	COLOR
■	310	◪		403	black
◉	347			1025	dk salmon
✚	367			217	dk green
♡	368	◪		214	lt green
◎	676	◪		891	gold
✛	677	◪		886	lt gold
✿	729			890	dk gold
	938		◪	381	mocha
▢	3328	◪		1024	salmon
●	938			381	mocha Fr. Knot

CROSS-STITCHED SNOWMAN BAG (page 21)

X	DMC	¼X	B'ST	ANC.	COLOR
·	B5200				white
■	304			1006	red
■	310		◪	403	black
✚	334			977	blue
✿	562			210	green
‖	563			208	lt green
Σ	676	◪		891	gold
✳	677			886	lt gold
✕	762			234	pearl grey
♡	818			23	lt pink
●	840			379	beige
2	841			378	lt beige
◺	842			388	vy lt beige
✿	938	◪	◪	381	dk brown
◉	3325	◪		129	baby blue
Ø	3801				salmon
●	310			403	black Fr. Knot
●	938			381	dk brown Fr. Knot

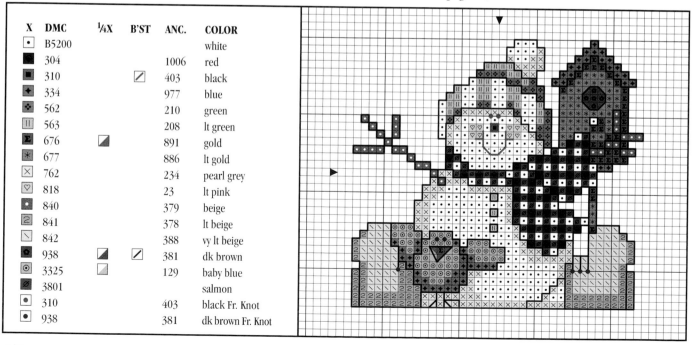

APPLIQUÉD NUTCRACKER BAG

(page 28)

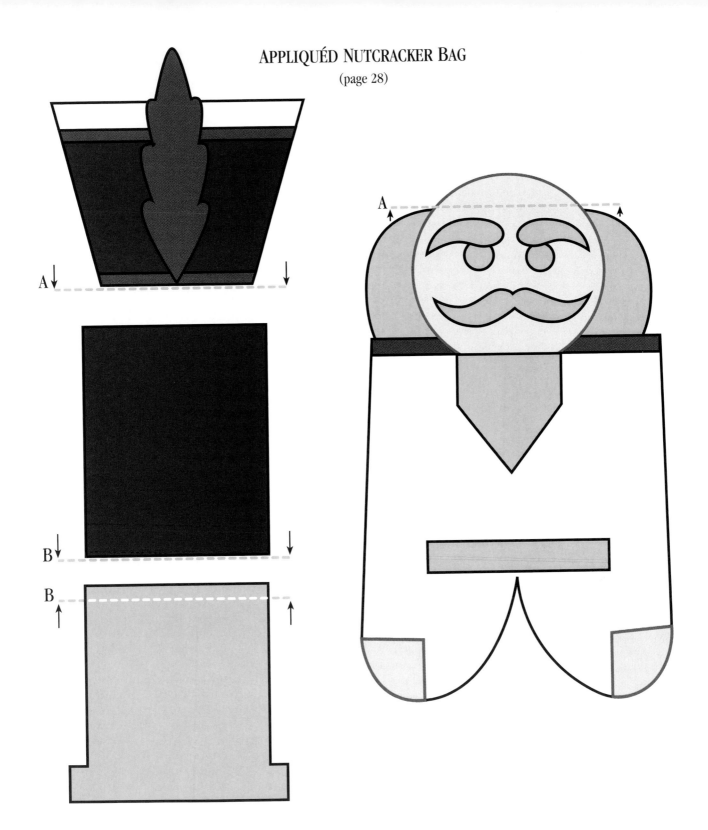

Happy New Year

COFFEE-BEAN POT
(page 121)

PAINTED FLOWER BAG
(page 116)

SPONGE-
PAINTED TIN
(page 96)

SNOWMAN MUGS
(page 8)

In the meadow we can build a...

PATTERNS (continued)

SPOOKY SPIDER BOTTLE
(page 124)

square

stem

olive

tomato

Pumpkin Boo Juice!

Bruschetta

*Leisure Arts, Inc., grants permission to the
owner of this book to photocopy the labels on
this page for personal use only.*

FOOTBALL BAG
(page 104)

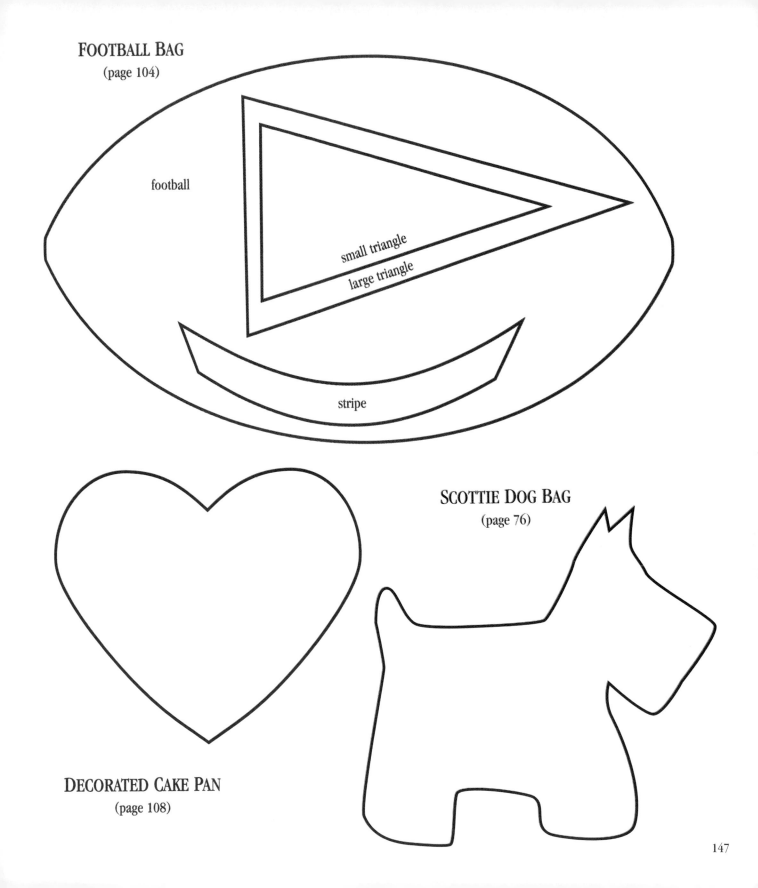

football

small triangle

large triangle

stripe

SCOTTIE DOG BAG
(page 76)

DECORATED CAKE PAN
(page 108)

PATTERNS (continued)

APPLIQUÉD PUMPKIN TINS
(page 126)

TURKEY CAN
(page 129)

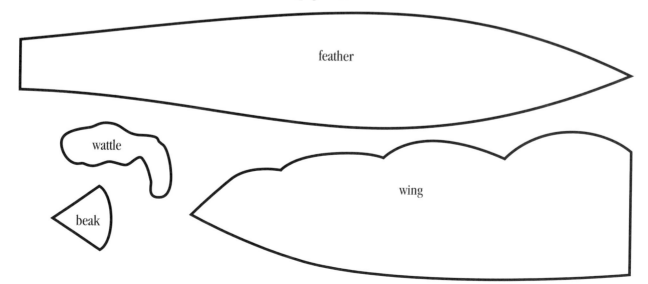

feather

wattle

beak

wing

JUST FOR YOU

NORTH POLE
Merry Meal

to:

from:

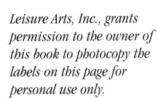

Leisure Arts, Inc., grants permission to the owner of this book to photocopy the labels on this page for personal use only.

To

From

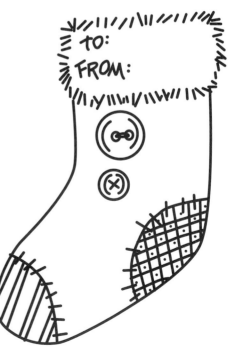

TO:

FROM:

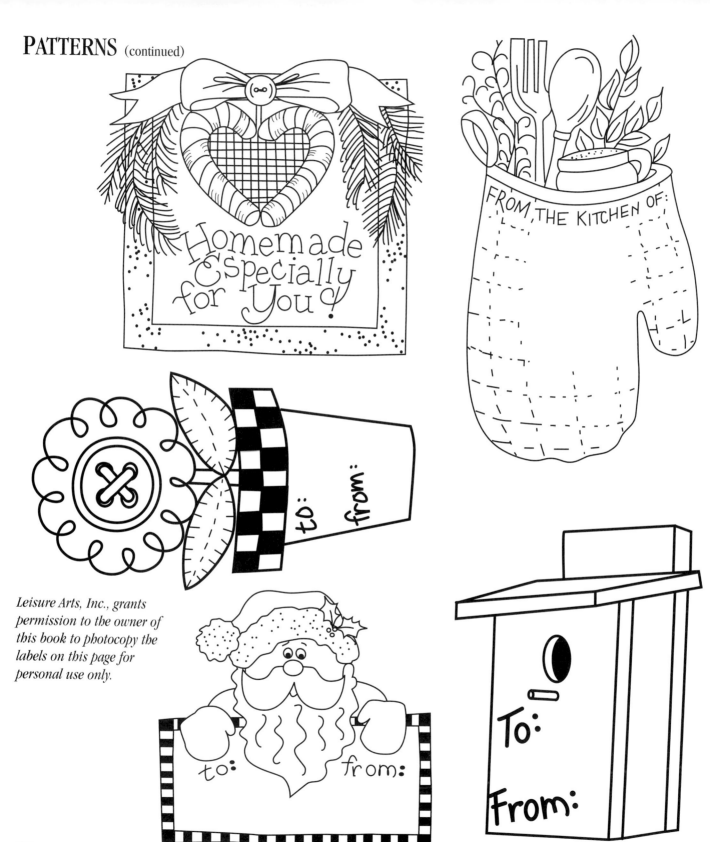

From, the Kitchen of:

Homemade Especially for You!

to:
from:

Leisure Arts, Inc., grants
permission to the owner of
this book to photocopy the
labels on this page for
personal use only.

to: from:

To:

From:

GENERAL INSTRUCTIONS

ABOUT THE PAPER WE USED

For many of the projects in this book, we used white and colored paper. There are a variety of papers for these projects available at copy centers or craft stores. When selecting paper, choose one that is suitable in weight for the project. We used copier paper, card and cover stock, construction paper, poster board, bristol board, and handmade paper.

ABOUT ADHESIVES

Refer to the following list when selecting adhesives. Carefully follow the manufacturer's instructions when applying adhesives.

CRAFT GLUE: Recommended for paper, fabric, wood, and floral items. Dry flat or secure with clothespins or straight pins until glue is dry.

FABRIC GLUE: Recommended for fabric or paper items. Dry flat or secure with clothespins or straight pins until glue is dry.

HOT/LOW-TEMPERATURE GLUE GUN AND GLUE STICKS: Recommended for paper, fabric, and floral items; hold in place until set. Dries quickly. Low-temperature glue does not hold as well as hot glue, but offers a safer gluing option.

CRAFT GLUE STICK: Recommended for small, lightweight items. Dry flat.

SPRAY ADHESIVE: Recommended for adhering paper or fabric items. Dry flat.

RUBBER CEMENT: Recommended for adhering paper to paper; dries quickly.

DECOUPAGE GLUE: Recommended for applying fabric or paper pieces to smooth surfaces.

HOUSEHOLD CEMENT: Used for ceramic and metal items; secure until set.

ADDING WELTING

1. Matching raw edges and ending 3" from end of welting, glue or sew welting to project. To make turning corners easier, clip seam allowance of welting at corners.

2. Fold fabric away and trim cord ends so that ends meet exactly (Fig. 1).

Fig. 1

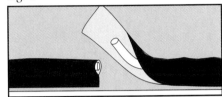

3. Fold short edge of welting fabric 1/2" to wrong side; fold fabric back over area where ends meet (Fig. 2).

Fig. 2

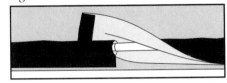

4. Glue or sew remainder of welting to project along edges.

CROSS STITCH

COUNTED CROSS STITCH (X):
Work one Cross Stitch for each colored square on chart. For horizontal rows, work stitches in two journeys (Fig. 1). For vertical rows, complete each stitch as shown in Fig. 2.

Fig. 1

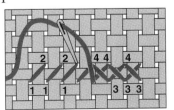

Fig. 2

BACKSTITCH (B'ST):
For outline or details, Backstitch (shown in chart and color key by colored straight lines) should be worked after the design has been completed (Fig. 3).

Fig. 3

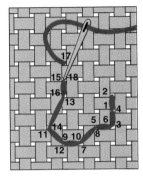

FRENCH KNOT
Bring needle up at 1. Wrap thread once around needle and insert needle at 2, holding thread with non-stitching fingers (Fig. 4). Tighten knot as close to fabric as possible while pulling needle back through fabric.

Fig. 4

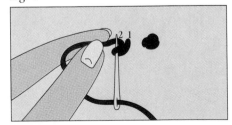

Continued on page 152

GENERAL INSTRUCTIONS (continued)

DECOUPAGE

1. Cut desired motifs from fabric or paper.
2. Apply decoupage glue to wrong side of each motif.
3. Arrange motifs on project as desired. Smooth in place and allow to dry.
4. Allowing to dry after each application, apply two to three coats of glue, varnish, or clear acrylic spray sealer over project.

EMBROIDERY STITCHES

LAZY DAISY STITCH

Bring needle up at 1 and go down at 2 to form a loop; bring needle up at 3, keeping thread below point of needle (Fig. 1). Go down at 4 to anchor loop (Fig. 2).

Fig. 1 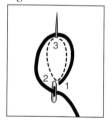 Fig. 2

RUNNING STITCH

Make a series of straight stitches with stitch length equal to the space between stitches (Fig. 3).

Fig. 3

STRAIGHT STITCH

Bring needle up at 1 and go down at 2 (Fig. 4). Length of stitches may be varied as desired.

Fig. 4

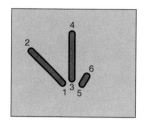

MAKING PATTERNS

When entire pattern is shown, place tracing paper over pattern and trace pattern; cut out. For a more durable pattern, use a permanent pen to trace pattern onto stencil plastic; cut out.

When only half of pattern is shown (indicated by blue line on pattern), fold tracing paper in half and place fold along blue line of pattern. Trace pattern half; turn folded paper over and draw over traced lines on remaining side of paper. Unfold paper and cut out pattern. For a more durable pattern, use a permanent pen to trace pattern half onto stencil plastic; turn stencil plastic over and align blue line with traced pattern half to form a whole pattern. Trace pattern half again; cut out.

When patterns are stacked or overlapped, place tracing paper over pattern and follow a single colored line to trace pattern. Repeat to trace each pattern separately onto tracing paper.

MAKING APPLIQUÉS

When tracing patterns for more than one appliqué, leave at least 1" between shapes on web.

To make a reverse appliqué, trace pattern onto tracing paper, turn traced pattern over, and follow all steps using traced pattern.

When an appliqué pattern contains shaded areas, trace along entire outer line for appliqué indicated in project instructions. Trace outer lines of shaded areas for additional appliqués indicated in project instructions.

1. Trace appliqué pattern onto paper side of web. (Some pieces may be given as measurements. Draw shape the measurements given in project instructions on paper side of web.) Cutting about 1/2" outside drawn lines, cut out web shape.
2. Follow manufacturer's instructions to fuse web shape to wrong side of fabric. Cut out shape along drawn lines.

MAKING A BASKET LINER

For liner with an unfinished edge, cut or tear a fabric piece 1/4" larger on all sides than desired finished size of liner. Fringe edges of fabric piece 1/4" or use pinking shears to trim edges.
For liner with a finished edge, cut a fabric piece 1/2" larger on all sides than desired finished size of liner. Press edges of fabric piece 1/4" to wrong side; press 1/4" to wrong side again. Stitch in place.

MAKING A BOW

Loop sizes given in project instructions refer to the length of ribbon used to make one loop.

1. For first streamer, measure desired length of streamer from one end of ribbon; twist ribbon between fingers (Fig. 1).

Fig. 1

2. Keeping right side of ribbon facing out, fold ribbon to front to form desired-size loop; gather ribbon between fingers (Fig. 2). Fold ribbon to back to form another loop; gather ribbon between fingers (Fig. 3).

Fig. 2   Fig. 3

3. (*Note:* If a center loop is desired, form half the desired number of loops, then loosely wrap ribbon around thumb and gather ribbon between fingers (Fig. 4). Continue to form loops, varying size of loops as desired, until bow is desired size.

Fig. 4

4. For remaining streamer, trim ribbon to desired length.

5. To secure bow, hold gathered loops tightly. Fold a length of floral wire around gathers of loops. Hold wire ends behind bow, gathering all loops forward; twist bow to tighten wire. Arrange loops and trim ribbon ends as desired.

PAINTING TECHNIQUES

TRANSFERRING A PATTERN

Trace pattern onto tracing paper. Using removable tape, tape pattern to project. Place transfer paper coated side down between project and tracing paper. Use a stylus or an old ball point pen that does not write to transfer outlines of base coat areas of design to project (press lightly to avoid smudges and heavy lines that are difficult to cover). If necessary, use a soft eraser to remove any smudges.

PAINTING BASE COATS

A disposable foam plate makes a good palette.

Use a medium round brush for large areas and a small round brush for small areas. Do not overload brush. Allowing to dry between coats, apply several thin coats of paint to project.

TRANSFERRING DETAILS

To transfer detail lines to design, replace pattern and transfer paper over painted base coat and use stylus to lightly transfer detail lines onto project.

ADDING DETAILS

Use a permanent pen to draw over detail lines.

SPATTER PAINTING

Cover work area with paper and wear old clothes when spatter painting. Before painting item, practice painting technique on scrap paper.

1. Place item on flat surface.
2. Mix 1 part paint to 1 part water. Dip toothbrush in diluted paint and pull thumb firmly across bristles to spatter paint on item. Repeat as desired. Allow to dry.

SPONGE PAINTING

Use an assembly-line method when making several sponge-painted projects. Place project on a covered work surface. Practice sponge-painting technique on scrap paper until desired look is achieved. Paint projects with first color and allow to dry before moving to next color. Use a clean sponge for each additional color.

For allover designs, dip a dampened sponge piece into paint; remove excess paint on a paper towel. Use a light stamping motion to paint item.

For painting with sponge shapes, dip a dampened sponge shape into paint; remove excess paint on a paper towel. Lightly press sponge shape onto project. Carefully lift sponge. For a reverse design, turn sponge shape over.

Continued on page 154

GENERAL INSTRUCTIONS (continued)

MAKING A FABRIC BAG

Bag may be hand-stitched, machine-stitched, glued or fused. Follow instructions below unless given specific measurements or different instructions in craft instructions.

1. To determine width of fabric needed, add 1/2" to desired finished width of bag. To determine length of fabric needed, double desired finished height of bag; add 1 1/2". Cut a piece of fabric the determined measurements.

2. Matching right sides and short edges, fold fabric in half; finger press folded edge (bottom of bag). Using a 1/4" seam allowance, sew sides of bag together.

3. For bag with flat bottom, match each side seam of fold line at bottom of bag; sew across each corner 2" from point (Fig. 1).

Fig. 1

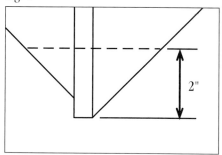

4. Press top edge of bag 1/4" to wrong side; press again 1/2" to wrong side and stitch in place.

5. Turn bag right side out.

MACHINE APPLIQUÉ

Place paper or stabilizer on wrong side of background fabric under fused appliqué. Set machine for a narrow zigzag stitch.

Beginning on a straight edge of appliqué if possible, position project under presser foot so that most of the stitching will be on the appliqué. Take a stitch in fabric and bring bobbin thread to top. Hold both threads toward you and sew over them for several stitches to secure; clip threads. Stitch over all exposed raw edges of appliqué(s) and along detail lines as indicated in instructions.

When stitching is complete, remove stabilizer. Clip threads close to stitching.

KITCHEN TIPS

MEASURING INGREDIENTS

Liquid measuring cups have a rim above the measuring line to keep liquid ingredients from spilling. Nested measuring cups are used to measure dry ingredients, butter, shortening, and peanut butter. Measuring spoons are used for measuring both dry and liquid ingredients.

To measure flour or granulated sugar: Spoon ingredient into nested measuring cup and level off with a knife. Do not pack down with spoon.

To measure confectioners sugar: Lightly spoon sugar into nested measuring cup and level off with a knife.

To measure brown sugar: Pack sugar into nested measuring cup and level off with a knife. Sugar should hold its shape when removed from cup.

To measure dry ingredients equaling less than 1/4 cup: Dip measuring spoon into ingredient and level off with a knife.

To measure butter, shortening, or peanut butter: Pack ingredient firmly into nested measuring cup and level off with a knife.

To measure liquids: Use a liquid measuring cup placed on a flat surface. Pour ingredient into cup and check measuring line at eye level.

To measure honey or syrup: For a more accurate measurement, lightly spray measuring cup or spoon with vegetable oil cooking spray before measuring so the liquid will release easily from cup or spoon.

TESTS FOR CANDY MAKING

To determine the correct temperature of cooked candy, use a candy thermometer and the cold water test. Before each use, check the accuracy of your candy thermometer by attaching it to the side of a small saucepan of water, making sure thermometer does not touch bottom of pan. Bring water to a boil. Thermometer should register 212 degrees in boiling water. If it does not, adjust the temperature range for each candy consistency accordingly.

When using a candy thermometer, insert thermometer into candy mixture, making sure thermometer does not touch bottom of pan. Read temperature at eye level. Cook candy to desired temperature range. Working quickly, drop about 1/2 teaspoon of candy mixture into a cup of ice water. Use a fresh cup of water for each test. Use the following descriptions to determine if candy has reached the correct stage:

Soft-Ball Stage (234 to 240 degrees): Candy can be rolled into a soft ball in ice water but will flatten when removed from water.

Firm-Ball Stage (242 to 248 degrees): Candy can be rolled into a firm ball in ice water but will flatten if pressed when removed from water.

Hard-Ball Stage (250 to 268 degrees): Candy can be rolled into a hard ball in ice water and will remain hard when removed from water.

Soft-Crack Stage (270 to 290 degrees): Candy will form hard threads in ice water but will soften when removed from water.

Hard-Crack Stage (300 to 310 degrees): Candy will form brittle threads in ice water and will remain brittle when removed from water.

SOFTENING BUTTER OR MARGARINE

To soften 1 stick of butter, remove wrapper and place butter on a microwave-safe plate. Microwave on medium-low power (30%) 20 to 30 seconds.

SOFTENING CREAM CHEESE

To soften cream cheese, remove wrapper and place cream cheese on a microwave-safe plate. Microwave on medium power (50%) 1 to 1 1/2 minutes for an 8-ounce package or 30 to 45 seconds for a 3-ounce package.

SHREDDING CHEESE

To shred cheese easily, place wrapped cheese in freezer 10 to 20 minutes before shredding.

TOASTING NUTS

To toast nuts, spread nuts on an ungreased baking sheet. Stirring occasionally, bake in a 350-degree oven 5 to 8 minutes or until nuts are slightly darker in color.

PREPARING CITRUS FRUIT ZEST

To remove the zest (colored outer portion of peel) from citrus fruits, use a fine grater or citrus zester, being careful not to grate bitter white portion of peel.

TOASTING COCONUT

To toast coconut, spread a thin layer of coconut on an ungreased baking sheet. Stirring occasionally, bake in a 350-degree oven 5 to 7 minutes or until coconut is lightly browned.

MELTING CANDY COATING

To melt candy coating, place in top of a double boiler over hot, not boiling, water or in a heavy saucepan over low heat. Stir occasionally with a dry spoon until

Continued on page 156

KITCHEN TIPS (continued)

coating melts. Remove from heat and use for dipping as desired. To flavor candy coating, add a small amount of flavored oil. To thin, add a small amount of vegetable oil, but no water. If necessary, coating may be returned to heat to remelt.

WHIPPING CREAM

For greatest volume, chill a glass bowl and beaters before beating whipping cream. In warm weather, place chilled bowl over ice while beating whipping cream.

SUBSTITUTING HERBS

To substitute fresh herbs for dried, use 1 tablespoon fresh chopped herbs for $1/2$ teaspoon dried herbs.

CUTTING OUT COOKIES

Place a piece of white paper or stencil plastic over pattern. Use a permanent felt-tip pen with fine point to trace pattern; cut out pattern. Place pattern on rolled-out dough and use a small sharp knife to cut out cookies. (*Note:* If dough is sticky, frequently dip knife into flour while cutting out cookies.)

MELTING CHOCOLATE

To melt chocolate, place chopped or shaved chocolate in top of a double boiler over hot, not simmering, water. Using a dry spoon, stir occasionally until chocolate melts. Remove from heat and use as desired. If necessary, chocolate may be returned to heat to remelt.

EQUIVALENT MEASUREMENTS

1 tablespoon	=	3 teaspoons
$1/8$ cup (1 fluid ounce)	=	2 tablespoons
$1/4$ cup (2 fluid ounces)	=	4 tablespoons
$1/3$ cup	=	$5^{1}/3$ tablespoons
$1/2$ cup (4 fluid ounces)	=	8 tablespoons
$3/4$ cup (6 fluid ounces)	=	12 tablespoons
1 cup (8 fluid ounces)	=	16 tablespoons or $1/2$ pint
2 cups (16 fluid ounces)	=	1 pint
1 quart (32 fluid ounces)	=	2 pints
$1/2$ gallon (64 fluid ounces)	=	2 quarts
1 gallon (128 fluid ounces)	=	4 quarts

HELPFUL FOOD EQUIVALENTS

$1/2$ cup butter	=	1 stick butter
1 square baking chocolate	=	1 ounce chocolate
1 cup chocolate chips	=	6 ounces chocolate chips
$2^{1}/4$ cups packed brown sugar	=	1 pound brown sugar
$3^{1}/2$ cups unsifted confectioners sugar	=	1 pound confectioners sugar
2 cups granulated sugar	=	1 pound granulated sugar
4 cups all-purpose flour	=	1 pound all-purpose flour
1 cup shredded cheese	=	4 ounces cheese
3 cups sliced carrots	=	1 pound carrots
$1/2$ cup chopped celery	=	1 rib celery
$1/2$ cup chopped onion	=	1 medium onion
1 cup chopped green pepper	=	1 large green pepper

RECIPE INDEX

CREDITS

To Magna IV Color Imaging of Little Rock, Arkansas, we say *thank you* for the superb color reproduction and excellent pre-press preparation.

We want to especially thank photographers Larry Pennington, Mark Mathews, and Ken West of Peerless Photography, Little Rock, Arkansas, for their excellent photography.

To the talented people who helped in the creation of the following projects and recipe in this book, we extend a special word of thanks:

- *Angel Ornament Basket*, page 16: Deborah Lambein
- *Cross-Stitched Snowman Bag,* page 21: Deborah Lambein
- *"Believe" Cross-Stitched Towel*, page 53: Jennifer Lambein
- *Cookie Basket*, page 68: Deborah Lambein
- *Teacher's Gift Ensemble,* page 94: Holly Witt
- *Fudge Brownies*, page 100: Mary Alice McDermott
- *Coffee-Bean Pot,* page 121: Holly Witt

Thanks also go to Ruth Ann Epperson, who assisted in making and testing projects in this book.